Maritime Firsts:

Historic Events, Inventions & Achievements

Dan Soucoup

Pottersfield Press
Lawrencetown Beach, Nova Scotia, Canada

Canadian Cataloguing in Publication Data

Soucoup, Dan, 1949–
    Maritime firsts
    ISBN 0-919001-97-1
1. Maritime Provinces — History. 2. Maritime Provinces — Miscellanea.
I. Title
FC2028.S64 1996   971.5   C95-950341-2
F1035.8.S68 1996

Front cover illustration: County map of Cape Breton, Nova Scotia, New Brunswick. and Prince Edward Island. (Augustus Mitchell, 1867)

Pottersfield Press gratefully acknowledges the ongoing support of the Nova Scotia Department of Education, Cultural Affairs Division, as well as the Canada Council and the Department of Canadian Heritage.

Printed in Canada

Pottersfield Press
Lawrencetown Beach
R.R. 2 Porters Lake
Nova Scotia, Canada, B0J 2S0

Dedication

For Joan, whose patience made this possible

Acknowledgments:

Halifax City Regional Libraries (including the Reference Library)
Public Archives of Nova Scotia
York County Regional Library
Provincial Archives of New Brunswick
Saint John Public Library
New Brunswick Museum
Island Institute of Prince Edward Island
Confederation Centre Public Library
Metro Toronto Reference Library

Contents

Introduction

"With great determination, 'Acadian' and 'Nova Scotian' pioneers have handed on a remarkable North American 'First Things' inheritance and it is up to posterity to enlarge and extend the sphere of human knowledge." — John Quinpool, First Things In Acadia.

This is a book about the Maritimes, primarily about the people and events that shaped the region into what it is today. While it is true that what happened here also happened throughout the Western World, I want to show that, despite popular opinion, it didn't always happen elsewhere first.

My idea for this chronicle of first achievements began one day while browsing through a book in the Halifax City Library. I couldn't help but notice the large number of Maritime entries in J.J. Brown's Ideas in Exile, A History of Canadian Invention. Almost all categories of inventions up to about 1900 included many Maritime contributions that I had never heard of. When I then went through Quinpool's First Things in Acadia and realized the astonishing number of unique events and innovations that happened here, my interest increased. The contributions indeed appeared numerous and seemed out of proportion to the region's small size and tiny population. I wasn't sure why.

I found myself searching through books and documents in libraries and archives, trying to substantiate a whole host of claims and counter claims about who did what where, and when, and if so, did it really happen here first? My approach was to try and get at least two distinct confirmations from sources that I considered reliable. Otherwise the item probably couldn't be confirmed and listed, at least not in any kind of authoritative way. Some of the entries may seem frivolous or humorous in comparison to the more serious contributions, yet all items are part and parcel of our history.

I'm hopeful that I've given the reader a bit more than a lot of facts and dates to remember. While the Maritimes may not have always been at the centre of North America's development, it did play an important and critical role, influencing and shaping events throughout the northern hemisphere. As we know, historically, Halifax and Louisbourg were the keys to the great English-French struggle for control of North America and this conflict, so devastating to the Acadians and Maritime aboriginals, was played out here, at Annapolis, Grand Pré, Beauséjour, and finally at Louisbourg itself.

While writing *Maritimes Firsts*, I often found myself trying to visualize what the Maritimes would have been like years ago, especially what it would have looked like during the hectic shipbuilding era of the square-rigged vessels. While standing with a colleague one evening at Chubbs Corner in Saint John, I tried imagining what the heydays of the 1840s would have been like with thirty or forty windjammers in port, loading and unloading cargo to and from the four corners of the globe. The scene would have included merchants in formal wear, half-starved immigrants jostling with sea captains and sailors from the tropics, men with wheelbarrows and horses fighting for space along the docks and narrow streets. Undoubtedly it was a very colourful scene, and quite different from today's quiet and often empty waterfronts throughout the Maritimes.

On another occasion, sailing out of Yarmouth harbour to Maine one September, I kept thinking about what old John Patch would have experienced trying to develop his invention. As we passed the docks and derelict wharfs, I wondered if Yarmouth's forgotten inventor would have been made a millionaire or a national hero if he had produced the world's first marine screw propeller system in Boston, London, or some other bustling seaport instead of the small Maritime port where he ended his days, sick in the town's poorhouse. Without financial resources, innovations were rarely successful. Perhaps the 1830s are too far away to ever get a real sense of what an inventor would have had to go through in those days. Yet if a pattern can be sketched out of *Maritime Firsts*, it is the continued realization that great ideas, once shown to work, often went nowhere.

Success seems to have been related to how well the Maritimer innovator was linked to the financial community. Men like Harry Chestnut in Fredericton, Forman Hawboldt in Chester, Graham in Pictou County, or Wallace Turnbull in Saint John either had funds or had access to capital in order to

Advertisement for the Starr Manufacturing Company's invention, the world's first steel, self-fastening skate.

successfully develop and market their ideas. Those without money or unable to convince a local financier to back a promising project were left with an idea that would probably be exploited elsewhere. However, if the inventor was determined enough, like Abraham Gesner, the technical breakthrough was exported and developed outside the region by the original inventor.

In *Maritime Firsts*, you will find a wide array of Maritime inventions, innovations, achievements and risk-taking that took place here. Some of these success stories may seem out-of-character with what we know, or think we know, about the present-day Maritimes. In working with this material, I became fascinated with these unusual characters who were able to contribute to our technical knowledge and somehow generate economic activity from so many remote Maritime locations.

I also came away with an admiration and awe for the Maritime communities where these innovators worked and lived, especially the nineteenth century towns and villages that seemed so full of vigour and excitement about anything that was new and could improve daily life. For example, Benjamin Tibbets must have caused considerable excitement in Fredericton when he demonstrated his compound steam engine, stirring a sceptical Saint John River bank crowd into a cheering frenzy. It would have been equally fascinating to witness the mob scene surrounding Chester harbour when Forman Hawboldt successfully demonstrated his new single-stroke gasoline engine.

Sports events as well produced spectacular crowds of spectators. The Kennebecasis River sculling re-match featuring the Paris-Tyne crews drew a "sea of humanity," as thousands of Saint John sport fans poured into Rothesay. Johnny Miles' homecoming at North Sydney, after winning his first Boston Marathon, drew thousands of well-wishers from all over Cape Breton.

Maritimes Firsts is a book of Maritime history that highlights key events and influential people that have pushed the region in new directions. I am sure that further research will unearth more innovations and firsts beyond those documented here. Perhaps additional study might well challenge some of my conclusions or point out errors and omissions. Certainly our full list of accomplishments is yet to be realized.

Chronology

10,000 B.C. The first aboriginal people appear in the Maritime region.

1497   The first known European to visit the North American mainland, John Cabot, lands at Cape North, Cape Breton.

1583   First known shipwreck in Canadian waters, Sir Humphrey Gilbert's *Delight*, goes down off Sable Island.

1604   First European settlement above Florida is established on the St. Croix River.
— The first skating in North America takes place during De Monts' winter expedition on the St. Croix River.

1605   First permanent European settlement at Port Royal.

1606   The first wheat is successfully grown at Port Royal.
— Louis Hébert, the first European doctor in Canada, arrives at Port Royal.
— Marc Lescarbot launches the first European theatre performance in North America at Port Royal.
— Matthew Da Costa arrives at Port Royal, the first known Black person in North America.
— The first European boat is also constructed at Port Royal.

1607   America's first grist mill is erected near Port Royal at Lequille.

1610   Jessé Fléché arrives at Port Royal becoming the first Roman Catholic missionary in Canada. He baptizes Mi'kmaq chief Henri Membertou.
— Madame Marie Hébert also arrives at Port Royal, the first white woman in Canada.

1611   The first Jesuits arrive at Port Royal.

1612   North America's first sawmill is erected at Lequille.

1626   Nova Scotia's Coat of Arms is issued by Charles I.

1630   Acadian dykelands are established around Port Royal by means of the aboiteau.

1632   The first school in Canada opens at Port Royal.
—Nicolas Denys starts Canada's first commercial lumber operation on the LaHave River.

Maritime Firsts

1643   Coal is first mined in North America near Minto.

1710   General Nicholson captures Port Royal and renames it Annapolis Royal, the first permanent British settlement in what becomes British North America.
— The first Church of England service in Canada is held at Annapolis Royal.

1720   Coal is first mined commercially at Port Morien to supply Louisbourg.

1727   Richard Watts begins the first English school in Canada at Annapolis Royal.

1734   First lighthouse in Canada shines at Louisbourg.

1744   Louisbourg becomes the first completely walled town in North America.

1749   Canada's first eighteenth century British colony is founded at Halifax.

1750   First German settlers in Canada arrive at Halifax.
— The first Protestant Church in Canada, St. Paul's, is constructed in Halifax.
— Major Lawrence erects the oldest blockhouse still standing in Canada, at Fort Edward.
— The first Board of Trade in Canada is founded in Halifax.
— The first legal divorce in Canada is issued at Halifax.

1751   Chabert de Cogolin erects earliest astronomical observatory in North America at Louisbourg.
— Canada's first printing press arrives at Halifax from Boston.
— Joshua Mauger builds the first rum distillery in Canada.

1752   Longest running saltwater ferry service in North America is established between Halifax and Dartmouth by John Conner.
— *Halifax Gazette* becomes the first newspaper published in Canada. The first eight-page booklet and first bilingual publication also appear.

1753   The *Halifax Gazette* publishes the first advertisement by a doctor in Canada.

1754   Benjamin Leigh opens Canada's first post office in Halifax.
— Halifax's St. Paul's Church is the site of the first Protestant orphanage in Canada.
— The first Presbyterian Church in Canada is built at Lunenburg.

1755   Governor Lawrence orders the expulsion of the Acadians.

1756   The Little Dutch Church in Halifax is erected, the first Lutheran Church in Canada.
— Halifax currency is established.

1758   The first Representative Parliament in Canada opens at Halifax.
— The Nova Scotia Legislature issues the first divorce statue in Canada.

1759   Nova Scotia becomes the first province in Canada to divide itself into counties.

1760   The oldest existing lighthouse in Canada is constructed on Sambro Island at the mouth of Halifax Harbour.

1761   James Rivington opens Canada's first English-language bookstore in Halifax.
— Ebenezer Moulton settles in Yarmouth, the first Baptist minister in Canada.
— Anthony Henry prints the first parliamentary journal in Canada.

1763   The first Baptist Church in Canada is established at Sackville.

1765   The old Meeting House at Barrington is constructed, the oldest existing Nonconformist Church in Canada.
— The first known agricultural fair in Canada is held at Windsor.

1768   First English-language drama is staged in Canada at Halifax.
— The first branch of the North British Society outside Britain is founded at Halifax.

1770   First Canadian almanac, *The Nova Scotia Calendar*, is printed by Anthony Henry.
— The first Presbyterian ordination in Canada is held at Lunenburg.
— First permanent colony of Highland Scots arrive at Prince Edward Island.

1773   Joseph Frederick DesBarres completes the first systematic survey of the east coast of North America.

1774   *Acadius*, the first English Canadian play written and performed in Canada, opens in Halifax.

1776   Canada's first female printer, Margaret Draper, arrives in Halifax from Boston.

1777   The first print illustration to appear in a book in Canada is printed by Anthony Henry.

1778   The first Baptist ordination in Canada is held at Wolfville.

1779   Flora MacDonald, the exile from Culloden, winters at Fort Edward.

1780   First Canadian poems printed in Canada, Henry Alline's *Hymns*, are released in Halifax.

1783   Congregation of the first Black Baptist Church in Canada meets at David George's home in Shelburne.

1784   The first race riot in Canada takes place at Shelburne.
— First British inland postal route is established between Quebec City and Halifax.
— New Brunswick becomes a separate province.

Maritime Firsts

1785   Saint John becomes the first incorporated city in British North America.
— Saint John's common-law market is also incorporated into its city charter.
— The city witnesses the first political riot in Canada.
— The oldest college in Canada is founded, the University of New Brunswick.

1786   The first marine insurance company in British North America is formed, the Halifax Marine Society.
— Canada's first Charitable Irish Society gathers in Halifax.

1787   The Halifax Chess, Pencil and Brush Club, the first artist's organization in Canada, is formed.
— Printer Anthony Henry issues the first ethnic publication in Canada, a German almanac.

1788   Anthony Henry renames his newspaper the *Royal Gazette* as he receives the first official King's Printer commission in British North America.

1789   Canada's oldest chartered university, King's College, is founded at Windsor.
— The Grand Theatre opens in Halifax, the first theatre in Canada.
— John Zwicker establishes the oldest fish company in Canada at Lunenburg.
— The first Canadian periodical is published in Halifax.

1791   New Brunswick's first lighthouse is erected on Partridge Island in the harbour of Saint John.

1792   Black Loyalist and preacher David George arrives in Sierra Leone, the first Baptist missionary to Africa.

1794   First Canadian-born English-speaking poet, Oliver Goldsmith, is born at St. Andrews.

1796   Prince Edward begins construction on the first Martello Tower in the British Empire at Point Pleasant Park. He also establishes the first semaphore telegraph system in North America.

1805   Oldest standing courthouse in Canada is erected at Tusket in southwestern Nova Scotia.

1809   The first Canadian fire insurance company is formed in Halifax.

1810   The oldest pharmacy in Canada opens at Charlottetown.

1812   The Saint John River's unique working boat, around since about 1790, is now called the woodboat.
— Charles Ramage Prescott, the apple pioneer, arrives at Starrs Point.

1813   P.E.I.'s holey dollars are cut.

1819   The oldest legislature building still in use in Canada, Province House, opens at Halifax.
— The first English-speaking Catholic seminary opens in Halifax.

1820   The Bank of New Brunswick becomes the first chartered bank in Canada.

1822   The first shipment of deals lumber leaves Saint John.

1823   *Letters of Mephibosheth* is released, considered the first Canadian work of humour.
— Mary Crowell Hichens and her husband move to Seal Island in southwestern Nova Scotia, establishing Canada's first lifesaving station.

1824   First Canadian novel to be written and published in Canada, *St Ursula's Convent* by Fredericton's Julia Beckwith Hart, is released.
— Thomas Rankine starts Canada's first biscuit factory in Saint John, producing mariner's hard tack.

1825   The first Trappist monastery in North America is built at Monastery.
— Canada's first policewoman, Rose Fortune, begins patrols on the waterfront of Annapolis Royal.

1826   Canada's first sailing regatta takes place at Halifax.
— Saint John circulates tenders for the first paid police force in British North America.

1829   Canada's oldest university building still in use, the Old Arts Building, is completed at Fredericton.

1830   Canada's first quarantine station at Partridge Island, established by charter in 1785, erects its quarantine hospital.
— The first public exhibition of art in British North America opens at Dalhousie College.

1832   John White prints the first Bible in Canada.

1833   The steamer *Royal William* completes the Pictou to England voyage, the first transatlantic crossing without the use of sail.

1834   John Patch demonstrates his screw propeller aboard the schooner Royal George in the Bay of Fundy.

1836   Canada's oldest public gardens, the Halifax Public Gardens, is opened by the Nova Scotia Horticultural Society.
— *The Clockmaker* by Thomas C. Haliburton, the first Canadian work to achieve international acclaim, is released in book form.
— Canada's first asylum for the mentally ill opens in Saint John.

1837   The first yacht club in Canada is organized on Halifax's Northwest Arm.
— James Robb teaches the first Canadian university course in chemistry at the University of New Brunswick.

1837   Abraham Gesner is appointed New Brunswick's first Provincial Geologist.

1838   The first penny newspaper in Canada is published at Saint John.

1839   Tristram Halliday opens Canada's first commercial canned food factory outside Saint John.
— *The Samson* locomotive arrives in Pictou County becoming the first train in North America to burn coal and run on all-rail tracks.
— Samuel Cunard starts the first steamer mail packet service between London, Halifax, and Boston.

1840   Halifax's William Cunnabell becomes the first printer in Canada to apply steam to his metal printing press.
Miners strike at the Albion Mine, the first coal strike in Canada.
— Canada's first balloon ascension takes place at Saint John.

1841   Charles Fenerty succeeds in producing paper from pulp wood at Upper Sackville, Nova Scotia.
— Saint Mary's University opens, becoming the first English Catholic university in Canada.

1842   William Valentine establishes the first photographic studio in Canada at Halifax.
— The Fraser brothers of Pictou, using a diver's helmet, undertake the first underwater salvage operation in Canada, off Prince Edward Island.
— The first public museum in Canada opens at Saint John.

1844   John P. Mott & Co. of Dartmouth is established as Canada's first chocolate company.

1845   Benjamin Tibbets constructs the *Reindeer* at the mouth of the Nashwaak River, installing the world's first compound steam engine.
— North America's first new British cathedral foundation is started at Fredericton.

1846   At Charlottetown, Abraham Gesner demonstrates his new kerosene fuel.

1847   Andrew Downs starts North America's first zoological gardens outside Halifax.
— Dr. Daniel McNeill Parker becomes the first physician in Canada to operate with the help of anesthesia.

1848   The first responsible government in Canada is formed at Halifax.
— Dr. William James Almon becomes the first Canadian doctor to administer chloroform in a Halifax hospital. The anesthetic is produced by the celebrated Pictou druggist, J.D.B. Fraser.

1849   The first waterfront worker's union in Canada is formed at Saint John.
— First foreign office of the Associated Press is established at Halifax.

Chronology

1851   The *Marco Polo* sets a world record sailing the round trip between England and Australia in under six months.

— Canada's oldest standing astronomical observatory is erected by William Brydone Jack at the University of New Brunswick in Fredericton.

— Brydone Jack also delivers the first public lectures on astronomy.

1852   St. Andrews constructs a hotel and becomes Canada's first seaside resort town.

— First undersea telegraph cable in North America is laid between New Brunswick and Prince Edward Island.

1853   Francis Peabody Sharp, Canada's first modern horticulturalist, introduces his new apple varieties at Upper Woodstock.

— Donald McKay of Jorden Falls, Nova Scotia launches the *Great Republic*, the largest clipper ship ever built.

1854   Robert Foulis invents the steam fog horn and five years later installs it on Partridge Island.

— A university course in civil engineering is taught for the first time in Canada at the University of New Brunswick.

1856   George T. Taylor begins his photographic career in Fredericton, pioneering nature photography in Canada.

1857   Nova Scotian Thomas Beamish Akins is appointed Canada's first Provincial Archivist.

1858   The only Canadian Prime Minister of Britain, Andrew Bonar Law, is born at Rexton.

1859   Acadia University establishes the first alumni organization in Canada.

— William Hall is the first Canadian sailor to be awarded the Order of the Victorian Cross.

— Thomas Hall begins building his threshing machines in Summerside.

1861   Stellarton becomes the site of the first co-operative society store in Canada.

1863   The oldest continuing Highland Games in North America begins at Antigonish.

1864   Canada's first Tenant's League is organized on Prince Edward Island.

— The Farmer's Bank of Rustico is established as Canada's first client-owned credit union.

— Canada's first coal miner's union is organized at New Glasgow.

— Charlottetown is host to the first official conference leading to Confederation.

1866   Dartmouth's John Forbes patents the first steel spring skate in the world.

1867   The Paris Crew of Saint John wins the four-man World Sculling Championship.
— Canada's first student college newspaper begins publishing at Fredericton.

1869   Canada's oldest continually operating student college newspaper is founded at Halifax.

1870   The first YWCA in Canada is founded at Saint John.
— George Dixon, a boxing innovator and the first man to win world boxing titles in three divisions, is born at Africville.
— The first Tancook Whaler schooners appear around Mahone Bay.

1871   The Paris Crew's sculling rematch against England's Tyne Oarsmen takes place near Saint John on the Kennebecasis River.

1874   World's first railway flanger is invented at Fredericton.

1875   Halifax's James Creighton organizes and plays in what many people consider the first ice hockey game in Montreal.
— James Whelphey develops the Long Reach skate outside Saint John.
— Mount Allison's Grace Annie Lockhart becomes the first woman to graduate from a degree-granting college in the British Empire.

1877   The first iron bridge fabricated in Canada is installed at Elmsdale.

1878   The first paper box company in Canada begins production in Saint John.

1879   William Phillips of Saint John becomes the first Canadian to play major league baseball.

1880   Charles G.D. Roberts releases *Orion, And Other Poems*, launching Canada's first literary movement.
— First quintuplets in Canada are born at Little Egypt, Nova Scotia.

1882   Harriet Stewart of Mount Allison becomes the first woman in Canada to be awarded a Bachelor of Arts degree.
— Nova Scotia grants free education for the blind.

1883   Steel is first produced in Canada at Trenton by the Nova Scotia Steel and Coal Company.
— Saint John's Victoria Skating Rink is the host site of the first known indoor speed skating competition in Canada.
— Condensed milk is first produced in Truro under the Reindeer brand.
— Dalhousie Law School is founded, the first law school in the British Empire to teach common law.
— The first aerial photographs in Canada are taken in Halifax.

1884   The first all-steel bridge in Canada is erected at Saint John.
— Over Halifax Harbour, the first swing bridge in Canada is installed.

Chronology

1885   The Fuller Brush Man, Alfred C. Fuller, is born at Welsford in the Annapolis Valley.

1886   The oldest art gallery in Canada, Zwicker's Gallery, opens for business in Halifax's north end.

1887   Shelburne's Issac Crowell begins mass producing dories after introducing his dory clip knees.

1888   The English port of Liverpool receives the largest load of deals lumber on record, from Kent County, New Brunswick.

1892   North America's first Gaelic newspaper, *MacTalla*, appears in Sydney.
       — Lyman Archibald organizes the first basketball game in Canada at St. Stephen.

1894   Margaret Saunders releases *Beautiful Joe*, the first Canadian children's work to achieve international status.
       — St. Francis Xavier becomes the first Catholic co-educational college in North America.

1895   Red Rose Tea is offered for sale by Theodore Estabrooks at Saint John.
       — The first Canadian home and school association is founded by Mabel Bell at Baddeck.
       — Joshua Slocum begins his three-year voyage around the world.
       — Canada's first university art gallery opens at Sackville.

1896   Charles Dalton and Robert Oulton succeed in breeding the silver fox in captivity on Prince Edward Island.

1898   Canada's first biological fisheries research station is established at St. Andrews.

1899   The first bulk cargo of oil arrives in Canada at Halifax.

1900   Chester's Forman Hawboldt develops the Hawboldt two-cycle marine engine.
       — Ephram Atkinson begins constructing the Cape Island boat at Clark's Harbour, on Cape Sable Island.
       — The first IODE chapter in Canada is started at Fredericton.
       — The Dominion Iron and Steel Company produces the first steel in Cape Breton.

1901   Frederick Creed convinces the British Post Office to buy his Creed Teleprinter, establishing its worldwide reputation.
       — The longest covered bridge in the world is completed at Hartland.

1902   First permanent radio station in Canada is constructed at Glace Bay. The first transatlantic wireless message is sent to England.

Maritime Firsts

1902   Wallace Turnbull builds the first wind tunnel in Canada to conduct aviation experiments.

1903   The first consolidated school is opened at Middleton.

1904   Harry Chestnut acquires the Canadian patent for constructing the wood and canvas canoe.

1905   The first female naval ship commander in Canada, Isabel Janet MacNeil, is born at Halifax.
    — The tallest wooden church in North America is constructed at Pointe de l'Énglise, Nova Scotia.

1906   Marconi establishes Canada's first radio equipment manufacturing company in Glace Bay.
    — North America's first self-contained breathing apparatus are used in Glace Bay coal mines.

1907   The first power plant to develop electric power from coal at the mine-pit opens near Amherst.
    — Alexander Graham Bell forms the Aerial Experiment Association at Baddeck, pioneering the research team concept for technical work and conducting experiments.

1908   Alexander Graham Bell builds the most technically advanced hydrofoil boat, the *Dhonnas Beag*.
    — *Anne of Green Gables* is released, the first Canadian children's work with lasting international acclaim.
    — Port Morien becomes the site of the first Boy Scout troop in Canada.
    — The *James William* is launched at New Glasgow, the first all-steel sailing schooner constructed in Canada.

1909   The first airplane flight in the British Empire occurs at Baddeck, aboard the *Silver Dart* and is flown by J.A.D. McCurdy. Dolly MacLeod becomes the first woman in flight when she flies aboard the *Silver Dart*.

1910   James Ganong produces the first chocolate nut bar at St. Stephen.
    — Canada's own navy is established.

1911   Canada's Royal Naval College opens its doors on the Halifax waterfront.

1912   Saint John passes the first town planning act in Canada.
    — Mabel Bell establishes the first Montessori school in Canada at Baddeck.

1913   *Evangeline* is produced in Halifax, the first Canadian feature-length motion picture.

1915   John Daniel Logan teaches the first Canadian literature course at Acadia.

1916   Wallace Turnbull invents the variable pitch propeller at Rothesay.

1917   Canada's first National Historic Park is opened at Annapolis Royal.
    — Wendell Rogers downs the first Gotha bomber over France.

1918   The first Department of Health in Canada is established in New Brunswick.
    — The first Police union in Canada is organized at Saint John.
    — Seed potatoes are first exported from PEI.

1919   Bell's *HD-4* hydrofoil boat establishes a world speed record on Baddeck Bay.

1922   Frontier College is founded by Pictou County's Rev. Alfred Fitzpatrick.

1923   Winnifred Blair of Saint John receives the first Miss Canada award.

1926   Unknown Johnny Miles wins the Boston Marathon and establishes a new world record.
    — Dr. Archibald G. Huntsman begins to freeze food commercially, producing the frozen fish fillet.

1927   The Halifax Curling Club wins the first Canadian men's curling championships.

1928   Moses Coady and Jimmy Tompkins start the Antigonish Movement through the Extension Department of St. Francis Xavier University.

1932   I.Cameron Mackie at Dominion Steel & Coal in Sydney patents his shatter-free railway rails production technique.

1935   Canada's first co-operative housing project, Tompkinsville, is started.
    — Edna Lockhart Duncanson becomes Canada's first female professional baseball player.

1936   J. Frank Willis makes Canada's first on-site news broadcast from Moose River, Nova Scotia.

1939   The only Gaelic college in North America opens at St. Ann's, Cape Breton.
    — The first naval convoy leaves Halifax for Europe.

1941   Mount Allison offers the first Bachelor of Fine Arts degree in Canada.

1958   Fredericton's Willie O'Ree becomes the first Black hockey player to play in the NHL.

1959   The Coady International Institute begins teaching overseas students.

1962   Canada's largest marine centre for oceanography opens on the Bedford Basin.

1963   Volvo assembles the first European car in Canada at Dartmouth.
    — Canada's first law school to teach civil law in French opens at the Université de Moncton.

1966   Glace Bay's Men of the Deeps form the first coal miner's singing choir in North America.

1967   The first commercial heavy water plant opens at Glace Bay.

1968   Mike McIntosh of St. Francis Xavier University becomes the first undergraduate in Canada appointed to a university's board of directors.
— Official bilingualism is introduced in New Brunswick, the only province in Canada with equal language status for French and English.

1970   The first major oil spill in Canada occurs in Chedabucto Bay.
— The first Canadian to win seven North America paddling championships, Dartmouth's Chris Hook, retires from competitive paddling.
— Sydney police undertake the first legal police strike in Canada.
— The first televised broadcast of a provincial legislature in Canada occurs at Halifax.
— An oceanographic research vehicle, the *Batfish*, is designed at the Bedford Institute of Oceanology.
— A vessel from the Bedford Institute of Oceanology, the *CSS Hudson*, becomes the first ship to circumnavigated the Americas.

1973   Carrie Best wins the first annual National Black Coalition award.

1979   Antonine Maillet becomes the first Canadian to win the Prix Goncourt.

1984   North America first tidal electrical power plant opens at Annapolis Royal.
— Daurene Lewis becomes the first Black woman mayor in Canada.

1985   Canada's first factory freezer trawler, the *Cape North*, arrives in Lunenburg.

1987   Colonel Sheila Hellstrom becomes the first female brigadier-general in Canada.

1991   North America's first single malt distillery, Glenora Distillery, opens in Cape Breton at Glenville.

1992   Canada's first offshore oil is produced near Sable Island.

1993   Catherine Callbeck of Prince Edward Island becomes the first woman elected premier in Canada.

1995   New Brunswick's Romeo LeBlanc is appointed Canada's first Acadian governor general.

Historical Achievements

"Thus it is not surprising to find the entire area of the East Coast of Canada a fertile ground for inventions and innovations of all kinds. The long struggle with the greatest of all natural opponents, the sea, has developed that independence of mind and spirit for which Maritimers are famous." — J.J. Brown, *Ideas In Exile, A History of Canadian Invention*

Aboriginal Contributions

The Mi'kmaq and Maliseet people had long occupied the Maritime region at the time of European arrival and had developed a well-established culture. Their achievements and skills were impressive as they managed to live and prosper in the wilderness by adapting materials from their harsh yet rich environment. Along with other peoples of the Eastern Woodlands, the Maritime aboriginals created the **birchbark canoe, snowshoes**, and **toboggan** for travel. They also developed the **tumpline**, often needed in their semi-nomadic lifestyle.

Working with simple but durable stone tools, along with natural elements such as wood, reeds, birchbark, porcupine quills, and rawhide, the first peoples of the Maritimes used their artistic skills to fashion a highly developed and decorative material culture. Extensive plant and animal knowledge allowed for good health throughout the seasons. Living lightly off abundant resources necessary for survival, these people continually tapped the rich forests, rivers and marshlands for thousands of years without exhausting nature's bounty.

The natural environment also provided the medicinal and spiritual basis for the aboriginals traditional way of life, allowing a culture to exist in balance and harmony with other unthreatened life forms.

As the first to experience extensive contact with Europeans in the sixteenth century, Maritime aboriginals became threatened with disease, war, and cultural change that radically altered their way of life. Despite tremendous struggles against centuries of white neglect, native peoples have provided many important contributions to modern civilization and today insist on regaining their former sovereignty. With renewed confidence and belief in their traditional forms of knowledge and community, a political and cultural renaissance is taking place.

European Settlements

Samuel de Champlain and Pierre Du Gua De Monts established the first **European settlement** in North America north of Florida on June 26, 1604 on an island lying at the mouth of the St. Croix River. Called l'île Sainte Croix and later Dochet Island, the small two-hectare (5 acre) site on the New Brunswick–Maine border, became the Europeans' first winter home and the foundation of the French colony of Acadia. Champlain and De Monts erected buildings, planted gardens, and outlined a plan for a permanent settlement, but during the first winter over half of the settlers died of scurvy.

The small island lacked fuel, good soil, fresh water and offered little protection against the elements. The following spring, the settlement moved across the Bay of Fundy to Port Royal. The exact location of Dochet Island was in dispute until 1797, when an excavation group, headed by Loyalist Ward Chipman, found the remains of Champlain's camp. The island lay on the west side of the Webster–Ashburton Treaty line of 1842 and became part of the United States. Both Canada and the US, however, recognized the historical significance of the international site, and in 1904 residents of the St. Croix Valley erected a memorial commemorating the island as the birthplace of Acadia.

Port Royal is considered the first **permanent European settlement** in North America, and during the summer of 1605 De Monts built the Habitation which consisted of buildings grouped around a courtyard. The location, along the north shore of the Annapolis Basin near present-day Annapolis Royal, proved suitable for agriculture, allowing the tiny colony to sustain itself. The settlement became the site of an array of historical achievements recorded by both Champlain and chronicler Marc Lescarbot, between 1605 and 1607, when it was temporarily abandoned, and again between 1610 and its destruction in 1613 by English raiders.

The courtyard of the Habitation, Port Royal, Annapolis Basin.

Sketch of the courtyard of the re-created Habitation, Port Royal, first permanent European settlement north of Florida. (L.B. Jenson)

The earliest known **Black person** to appear in North America was Matthew Da Costa. He arrived in Acadia with Champlain in 1606 from La Rochelle, France aboard the *Jonas*. Knowledgeable in the Mi'kmaq and Maliseet dialects through a previous visit with the Portuguese, Da Costa served as Champlain's and De Monts' translator. A chartered member of the Order of Good Cheer, he died of scurvy at Port Royal the next winter.

Port Royal can lay claim to the first **agricultural gardens, apple orchards** and **grist mill, Acadian dykes**, as well as the first **European theatre, doctor, lawyer,** and **missionaries**. Even North America's first **European ships** were constructed there. After the fort's destruction, Acadian farmers slowly developed the area for agriculture, establishing a village upriver at what is now Annapolis Royal. Britain did not permanently dominate the region until the British General Francis Nicholson captured Port Royal in 1710.

The 1713 Treaty of Utrecht ceded Acadia to England, consequently Port Royal became Annapolis Royal, while the French fort was renamed Fort Anne. Annapolis Royal became the first **permanent British foothold** in what became British North America. The British required that Acadians who wished to remain swear an oath of allegiance to Queen Anne. The Habitation was reconstructed in 1939 at the original Port Royal site through federal efforts and the following year became a National Historic Park.

Ethnic Settlements

On September 2, 1750, Governor Edward Cornwallis announced to his Halifax council the arrival of the ship *Ann* from Rotterdam with three hundred "German" settlers aboard, the initial **German immigration** to Canada. While it is unclear if the immigrants included any Dutch, Swiss, or other European settlers, it seems certain that all had been declared Foreign Protestants. Cornwallis considered these European, non-Catholic settlers ideal for British settlement, capable of countering the French Catholic influence in Nova Scotia. They would also be loyal to Britain in her struggle for North America domination. Lunenburg became their destination and by 1753 almost 1,500 Foreign Protestants settled there, Canada's first **German community**.

Nova Scotia was also the first Canadian region to experience a major influx of Blacks when over two thousand **Black Loyalists** arrived at Shelburne in 1783. While Nova Scotia also received a large number of Scottish immigrants, the earliest **permanent Scottish Highland settlers** actually landed on Prince Edward Island, then called the Island of St. John. The Fraser Highlanders from the shires of Ross, Inverness, Sutherland, and Argyll arrived in 1770 on board the *Falmouth* from Greenock, on the Clyde River. Three years later, the ship *Hector* arrived at Pictou with almost two hundred Highland Scots, the beginning of the large-scale emigration of Scots to eastern Nova Scotia.

Coat of Arms and a Flag

In 1626 Nova Scotia became the first colony of Great Britain to receive its own **Coat of Arms and flag**. The Coat of Arms was granted by Charles I, only the second king to wear the united crowns of England and Scotland. The lion stands for Scotland and the unicorn England, while the shield contains the blue cross of St. Andrew, the patron saint of Scotland. The native stands for the province's first people, while the Latin motto reads, "With one hand he works and with the other he defends." The flag is derived from the Coat of Arms, but at Confederation a new coat was issued to Nova Scotia. In 1929, however, the original ancient Scottish emblazon was retrieved while London officially re-enacted and re-issued it to Nova Scotia.

James I of England, who was also James VI of Scotland, named Nova Scotia. In 1621 he granted the entire region to Sir William Alexander, the Scottish Earl of Stirling, calling it Nova Scotia as opposed to the competing French name Acadia. The Latin name Nova Scotia, meaning New Scotland, also complemented North America's other infant colonies, New England and New France. Sir William's son briefly established the first two Scottish settlements in North America at Annapolis Royal and in Cape Breton. But by 1632 a shortage of financial resources and French opposition forced their abandonment.

Astronomical Observatories

French naval officer and astronomer, Chabert de Cogolin, erected the earliest **astronomical observatory** in North America at Louisbourg in 1750-51. Chabert visited North America to correct French charts and maps of the Atlantic coastline. Establishing exact longitude was still a navigational puzzle in 1750 since point zero had still not been agreed upon. Chabert had made an earlier voyage to New France as navigator on the ill-fated Duc D'Anville's expedition. In order to accurately navigate along the North America coast, Chabert hoped to pinpoint the exact longitude of Louisbourg as the centre of French seapower in the New World.

Chabert de Cogolin arrived at Louisbourg aboard the frigate *La Mutine* with eight telescopes as well as a range of surveying and astronomical equipment. A small all-weather observatory was constructed on the south side of the King's Bastion. With his assistant, Diziers-Guyon, who specialized in geometry, Chabert undertook astronomical observations for more than a year. Chabert returned to France and published his finding with the French Royal Academy of Sciences. His hydrographic survey resulted in the most accurate navigational information then available about the east coast. The observatory remained in use with French cartographers until its destruction with the fortress in 1758.

The **oldest standing astronomical observatory** in Canada, the Brydone Jack Observatory, opened in 1851 on the University of New Brunswick campus at Fredericton. William Brydone Jack, a Scottish immigrant with a keen interest in applied sciences, established the first **university observatory** in Canada and also is reported to have delivered the first **public lectures in astronomy** in Canada at Fredericton in the same year. Assisted by Harvard University, Brydone Jack located the correct longitude of Fredericton and other New Brunswick sites, as well as correcting errors in the international Maine–New Brunswick boundary. Today the observatory is a museum, featuring surveying equipment and a German-made mahogany and brass telescope constructed in 1849.

Oldest Standing Courthouse

Argyle Township Courthouse and Gaol was built in the southwestern Nova Scotia village of Tusket, near Yarmouth, between 1801 and 1805 and is considered the **oldest standing courthouse** in Canada. The old jail cells and jail-keeper's room are located on the ground floor while the court and jury room, as well as the judge's chamber, are situated on the second floor, overlooking the scenic Tusket River. A bell tower graces the old courthouse that offers guided tours during the summer months. Restored in 1982, the handsome structure now contains the area's historical archives.

Canada's First Policewoman

In 1825, Rose Fortune of Annapolis Royal became Canada's first **policewoman**, charged with keeping order on the town's wharf. A rare individual for her time, Rose Fortune was a Black female entrepreneur, who established a shipping business as a baggage handler, or "baggage smasher" as it was then called, shipping goods to and from Saint John, Boston, and Annapolis Royal.

Rose Fortune was born into slavery in the United States about 1774, the daughter of James Fortune who in 1783 arrived in the Annapolis Valley as a British Empire Loyalist, fleeing the American Revolution. As a pioneer Loyalist, Fortune and his family were described as free Negroes on the Annapolis muster roll of 1784. Rose settled in Lequille, outside Annapolis Royal, and actually began her transport business by carting a heavy wheelbarrow to the dock offering to off-load baggage for passengers arriving on the *Maid of the Mist* boat from Saint John. For a modest fee she would deliver luggage or cargo anywhere in Annapolis Royal.

A popular and unusual figure in Annapolis, Rose Fortune dressed eccentrically but was an energetic and reliable businesswoman who eventually acquired a monopoly on waterfront freight and was asked to also establish order. She ruled the waterfront with a strong arm and often accompanied prominent visitors to and from the town's hotel and the wharf. One of her best known friends was the famous author and judge, Thomas Haliburton, who resided in Annapolis Royal for eight years, nicknaming her affectionately "my Black Venus."

Rose Fortune's transport business became the Lewis Transfer Company in 1841, when her daughter married into the Lewis family. The company operated horse-drawn wagons and remained in the Lewis family until it was sold in 1965. In 1984, a relative of Rose Fortune, Daurene Lewis, became the mayor of Annapolis Royal, the first **female Black mayor** in Canada.

Public Gardens

Canada's oldest **public gardens**, the Halifax Public Gardens was opened in 1836 along Spring Garden Road by the Nova Scotia Horticultural Society. Intended as a city retreat "accessible to all classes," the Society was also interested in promoting horticulture and botany. Its original two hectares (5 acres) was purchased by the city in 1874, after having been merged with a nearby civil garden, and expanded to 6.5 hectares (16 acres). The nearby Halifax Commons comprises ninety-four hectares (232 acres) and was one of Canada's **first parks** when it was granted to the people of Halifax in 1763.

Designed by Superintendent Richard Power as a formal Victorian garden, the historic site includes geometric lawns, walks, serpentine paths, stone bridges, fountains, duck ponds, sculptures, exotic flower beds and a central bandstand gracing the magnificent array of botanical delights. A covered skating rink existed for about twenty years and the Soldier's Memorial was erected in 1903 to commemorate Canada's efforts in the Boer War. The Public Gardens was also the site of one of Canada's earliest public lawn tennis courts.

Few other Victorian gardens have survived throughout North America and in 1984 the Halifax Public Gardens was designated a National Historic Site. Descendants of the two swans presented to the Gardens in 1926 by King George V swim quietly in Griffin's Pond and over eighty different kinds of trees grow within the park, as well as at least three hundred varieties of shrubs and flowers. A set of high wrought iron gates from Scotland hang at the main Spring Garden Road entrance, while the other three entrances have smaller metal gates. Open to the public from May to November each year, the Public Gardens is one of Halifax's most popular attractions.

Zoological Gardens

The first **zoological gardens** in North America, north of Mexico, was started in 1847 by Andrew Downs, near the head of Halifax's Northwest Arm. Begun as a two-hectare (5 acre) retreat for Maritime wildlife, the Downs Zoo expanded within fifteen years to forty hectares (100 acres) and included a museum, aquarium, and greenhouse, as well as both native and exotic fauna. Downs began to stock the zoo with exotic creatures especially birds, from all over the globe, and attempted to house and display the beasts in their natural habitat. The exotic animals were shipped from far away ports and delivered to Halifax by the captains of the great square-rigger sailing ships.

Andrew Downs began his career as a plumber and his knowledge of zoology and taxidermy was largely self-taught, but he became well respected in his field and by 1846 became curator of the local Mechanics Institute. Downs won a number of zoological awards, including a silver medal in an 1867 stuffed bird exhibition in Paris. He claimed to have stuffed eight hundred moose heads during his lifetime.

Downs sold his animals and grounds in 1867 and briefly became the superintendent of the New York Zoo. First opened in 1853, the New York Zoological organization may have quarrelled with Downs, who reappeared in Halifax the same year, purchasing new land along the Arm and opening a smaller zoological gardens. An author of many articles on natural history, especially for the Zoological Society of London, Downs died in Halifax in 1892.

Quintuplets

Little Egypt, Pictou County, became the site of the first reported **birth of quintuplets** in Canada, when in 1880 hundreds gathered outside the home of Adam and Jeanette Murray to catch a glimpse of the five children. The largest of the small, but perfectly formed, three girls and two boys, weighed 1.8 kilograms (3 pounds, 14 ounces), while the smallest girl weighed 1.1 kilograms (2 pounds, 8 ounces). Unfortunately, this remarkable multiple birth ended in tragedy when all five children died within two days.

A controversy surrounded the attempted burial when large numbers of people were allowed to view the bodies lying in tiny rosewood caskets. The American showman P.T. Barnum offered a large sum of money in order to mummify the bodies for his travelling exhibitions. The Murray family declined but feared grave-robbers and held the bodies of the infants in their cellar until a secret burial place could be arranged.

Historic Resort

With the construction in 1852 of its first hotel, called The Inn, St. Andrews became Canada's first **seaside resort town**. Originally built to house the manager of the fledging New Brunswick & Canada Railway, The Inn was eventually purchased by the Canadian Pacfic Railway, along with the town's best known resort hotel, the Algonquin.

St. Andrews was established in 1783 by Loyalists and initially rivalled Saint John for shipbuilding and commerce. By the mid-1800s, its commercial base had declined and the town began to promote its location at the head of the cold waters of Passamaquoddy Bay as an ideal vacation destination for people living in the crowded and dirty cities of eastern North America.

Little was known at the time about disease, especially seasonal ills like flu and hay fever, and the notion of travelling to colder, quiet locations for cures and rest became popular with wealthy Americans in the northeastern United States. The resort town also claimed its cool summer breezes ensured the absence of mosquitoes and malaria. On Queen Victoria's birthday in 1881 two resort facilities opened, sealing St. Andrews' fate as Canada's premier seaside resort.

The Kennedy Hotel, now called the Shiretown Inn, and Hotel Argyll, which ran advertising posters and flyers citing its promise to tourists: "ABSO-

LUTE HAY FEVER EXEMPTION," became popular destinations. With establishment of rail connections to New England and Upper Canada and construction of the impressive Algonquin Hotel, St. Andrews By The Sea became a fashionable resort that continues to attract large numbers of visitors.

Canadian I.O.D.E.

The first Canadian chapter of the **Imperial Order Of the Daughters of the Empire** was established at Fredericton on February 1, 1900. The chapter was named Governor Carleton, and Mrs. John Black became its president with thirty-seven women initially registering. The idea for the organization originated in Montreal, but the Fredericton chapter quickly formed, raising $858.40 for the Patriotic War Fund destined for the Boer War in South Africa. This federation of women quickly expanded to over seven hundred chapters with branches in India, Bermuda and other Commonwealth countries as well as the United States.

Miss Canada

Winnifred Blair of Saint John received the **Miss Canada Award** in February 1923 at the first Miss Canada Pageant held in Montreal. Crowned at the ballroom of the Windsor Hotel during Montreal's Winter Carnival, Winnifred Blair returned by train to Saint John and arrived at Union Station amid cheering from thousands of supporters. The city turned out *en masse* to greet her with people waving flags and the local St. Mary's band enthusiastically rendering Oh Canada! Overwhelmed by the hometown welcome, Blair was paraded through the crowded streets to reign over an international skating meet.

Telegrams of congratulations were dispatched to Winnifred Blair from all over the Maritimes, as the successful candidate was treated to a royal welcome without parallel in Saint John's history. Blair later married the eminent Saint John lawyer Harold Drummie, who served as legal counsel to the Ganongs of St. Stephen, masterminding a brilliant legal defense during a hostile takeover attempt of their chocolate company in the 1940s.

Communication

"Halifax April 23, 1754
For the Benefit of the PUBLICK.
There Is now open'd at the first House without the South Gate, an
Intelligence and Outward POST-OFFICE viz . . . . .
Their Humble Servant
Benjamin Leigh"
— Newspaper advertisement for the first post office in Canada.

First Written Script

The earliest **written signs** in eastern North America were the hieroglyphs of the Mi'kmaq people. Initially inscribed on stone, birch bark, or wood, the Mi'kmaq writing system became central to their spiritual and cultural life. Once contact with French settlers and missionaries began, the hieroglyphs were expanded by Chrestien LeClercq and others to record the Catholic prayers and sacraments. These unique characters were often personally transcribed by each Mi'kmaq and treasured as their sacred prayer book. Today, only a small number of Mi'kmaq elders have retained hieroglyphic reading and writing skills.

Early Printing

Boston served as the early printing and publishing centre of the thirteen American colonies, so it's not surprising that the new Nova Scotian town of Halifax, only a few days northeast by sea, would become the printing centre of the British northern settlements.

The first **printing press** in Canada, a wooden common press, arrived by boat from Boston in 1751, after Bartholomew Green Jr. had heard that British authorities had neglected to include printing equipment with the materials sent out from England to found Halifax in 1749. Green had fought at

Richard Short's 1759 illustration of St. Paul's Church on Halifax's early Parade Square. Canada's first printing press is housed behind the church in John Bushell's printing office with weathervane perch. (Public Archives of Nova Scotia)

Louisbourg as a lieutenant of artillery and intended to establish a newspaper with his printing press but died within a month of reaching Nova Scotia. Green's family were Boston printers. His father, Bartholomew, in 1704 established the first newspaper in America, the *Boston Newsletter*. Green's Boston partner, John Bushell, arrived in Halifax shortly after Green's death and together with Anthony Henry pioneered early printing in Canada.

The first **female printer** in Canada was Margaret Draper, who was also part of the Green printing family and arrived in Halifax with her business partner, Loyalist John Howe. Draper had conducted a printing business in Boston with Howe that included publishing the Loyalist *Boston Newsletter*. When the British evacuated Boston in 1776, she accompanied Howe to Halifax and established a press. Howe seems to have bought her share of the printing business since she ended up moving to England. Joe Howe's father became the sole owner of the press and eventually, in 1800, was named King's Printer for Nova Scotia.

Halifax continued to be an important Canadian centre for printing and publishing until about Confederation. In 1840, William Cunnabell became the first printer in Canada to **apply steam power** to his all-metal Washington press imported from the United States. Cunnabell had served as printer's apprentice to the publisher of the *Acadian Recorder*, and in 1837 began publishing the *Nova Scotia Almanac*, featuring beautiful woodcuts. He also published the first **penny paper** in Nova Scotia as well as the Gospel of St. John in the Mi'kmaq language.

The first **Bible printed** in Canada was issued in Charlottetown in 1832 by printer John Henry White. White had arrived from Halifax intending to establish a rival newspaper to the semi-official *Royal Gazette*. He set up his stationery and printing business in the old Wellington Hotel on Great George Street. While printing the Bible was officially against British patent laws, colonial copyright laws were not strictly enforced and White is thought to have imported the printing plates from Boston. He advertised the Bible in his weekly paper, the *British American*, and offered to barter grain in exchange for payment. It is not known how many Bibles White printed, but 350 copies were auctioned after his death.

King's Printer

For its first ten years, Halifax had a single source for all its printing and publishing. John Bushell also acted as the government's printer, publishing official advertisements in his *Halifax Gazette* and printing government documents.

As unofficial King's Printer, Bushell in 1752 produced for Governor Hopson and Governor Duquesne of Quebec the earliest known **government document** printed in Canada. Called *A Cartel For the Exchange Of Deserters*, it guaranteed the reciprocal exchange of French and English deserters. The notice is also considered the first **bilingual publication** in Canada. Bushell printed the document in two columns with English text on the left and French on the right.

As well the first **booklet** published in Canada, a six-page pamphlet, in eight and ten-point type and italics, entitled *An Act for the Relief of Debtors* is generally considered to be from this period. Also printed by Bushell in 1752 for the government of Nova Scotia, a copy of the pamphlet is preserved at Acadia University. Bushell may have wanted to see the publication issued for personal reasons since he is reported to have had serious financial problems running his printing and publishing business in early Halifax.

John Bushell died in 1761 and his new partner, German printer Anthony Henry (Heinrich), continued to run the press and publish Bushell's newspaper. An army fifer with the Royal Americans regiment, Henry arrived in Halifax in 1758, working at Bushell's press. Henry also acted as unofficial King's Printer until an employee with republican interests, Isaiah Thomas, inserted items critical of the Stamp Act, the tax used to help pay for the British garrison. Thomas was dismissed and eventually deported to Boston for "seditious" actions.

Press censorship was enacted in 1766 by the Halifax authorities and Henry temporarily lost the paper and government patronage to Robert Fletcher, a new printer from London. Fletcher started another newspaper, the *Nova Scotia Gazette*, and a bookstore but eventually sold the press back to Henry.

In 1788, Henry received the official commission of **King's Printer**, the first in British North America, and renamed his paper the *Royal Gazette*. While not a particularly skillful printer, Anthony Henry worked hard at his craft for over forty years in early Halifax, pioneering many publications. In 1761 he produced the earliest **printed parliamentary journal** in Canada, the *Votes of the Nova Scotia House of Assembly*. Henry died in 1800 and is buried in St. Paul's cemetery.

Newspaper Publishing

Newspaper publishing began in Canada on March 23, 1752. The weekly *Halifax Gazette* was published on Grafton Street, near Duke Street, and consisted of a single two-column sheet with news and advertisements printed on both sides. Published by Bostonian John Bushell, Canada's first newspaper contained about one quarter local news, in addition to items copied from British and American newspapers.

The *Gazette* also contained proclamations and advertising for Halifax merchants and cost fifteen shillings per year. Advertisements publicized a reading school for children and beef at sixpence per pound. Bushell seems to have lost editorial control in about 1754 to Provincial Secretary Richard

Bulkeley, considered the first **newspaper editor** in Canada. Bushell continued to publish the *Gazette* until his death in 1761.

Anthony Henry continued Bushell's newspaper and in 1787 started Canada's first **German language publication** *Halifax Zeitung,* considered the first ethnic publication in Canada. The following year, Henry produced an almanac in German entitled *Der Neu-Schottlandische Calender Auf das Jahr Christi.* The German almanac was distributed to the German settlers at Lunenburg.

The first **almanac** printed in Canada was also published by Anthony Henry in 1770 as *The Nova Scotia Calendar.* The 1777 edition included a woodcut illustration of Halifax harbour, believed to be the earliest **print illustration** produced in a book in Canada.

Henry also established the first Canadian **newspaper to publish separately** from government patronage, the eight-page *Nova Scotia Chronicle and Weekly Advertiser,* which seems to have survived mainly from Whig support. In 1770, Henry merged the independent publication with the *Gazette* to become the *Nova Scotia Gazette and Weekly Chronicle.*

Halifax is also said to be the location of the first **college newspaper** in Canada. The first student newspaper, however, was actually began in 1867 at the University of New Brunswick through the efforts of student George Foster who later lectured at Fredericton. Foster's literary paper, the *University Monthly,* lasted only one year but was re-established in 1882. Later renamed *The Brunswickan,* it is still today UNB's official student publication.

Founded in 1869, the *Dalhousie University Gazette* is the oldest continually operating student college newspaper in Canada. Four pages long and costing five cents, its annual subscription rate cost fifty cents. The *Gazette* proclaimed a two-fold aim: "the cultivation of a literary taste and the establishment of an organ in which free expression can be given." Published by three Dalhousie students every alternate Monday, copies could be purchased at a Granville Street bookstore or from the college janitor.

The *Saint John Morning News,* published tri-weekly in Saint John in 1838, is cited as the first **penny newspaper** in the British Empire. The paper was started by George E. Fenety on Canterbury Street following word of similar successfully priced papers in the United States. Fenety had served as printer's apprentice to Joe Howe in Halifax and eventually became New Brunswick's Queen's Printer. Fenety charged one copper penny when local papers usually sold for ten cents. A great bargain and marketing innovation for its time, the *News* became the leading political paper in Saint John and later went daily, changing its name to *The Daily News*.

Although an issue in Gaelic of *The Young Highland Visitor* seems to have been published in Antigonish in 1851, North America's first **Gaelic newspaper**, *MacTalla*, was published in Sydney in 1892 by Gaelic scholar Jonathan G. MacKinnon of Dunakin-Whycocomagh, Cape Breton. Lasting twelve years, the paper carried local and international news as well as advertisements and correspondence of interest to the estimated twenty thousand Gaelic speakers in turn-of-the-century Cape Breton. MacKinnon also translated a number of English classics into Gaelic before his death in 1944 and taught at the first Gaelic college in North America. Gaelic is still alive today in eastern Nova Scotia, where at Mabou, Inverness County, the newspaper *Am Braighe* is published.

James Rivington, Bookseller

Bookselling began in North America when merchants and printers imported European books for a small group of readers, including garrison officers, merchants, and the clergy. By 1750 bookselling was well established in America and New France, but the first **English language bookstore** in British North America was not established until 1761.

James Rivington was a member of a well-known family of London booksellers. He first advertised his stock for sale in the May 14, 1761 issue of the *Halifax Gazette*. A year earlier, Rivington is known to have also opened a bookstore in New York together with a partner, William Brown, who later moved to Quebec and started its first newspaper as well as becoming the King's Printer at Montreal.

Rivington may have found business in the garrison town of Halifax slow, because soon after 1761 he moved to New England and is known to have established a chain of bookstores and printing presses throughout New England and New York. By 1766, another bookseller and printer, Englishman Robert Fletcher, had arrived in Halifax and sold books out of his establishment, which he advertised as Robert Fletcher On The Parade, Bookseller and Stationer. Fletcher also began to import and retail general merchandise, but his business skills were reported to have been poor and he too was not successful at bookselling, declaring bankruptcy in 1782.

Canada's First Postal Service

The Halifax **post office**, opened in April 1754 by schoolmaster, stationer, and auctioneer Benjamin Leigh, initially served as a pick-up depot for incoming mail and then as a somewhat irregular packet service to New York and England. Letters were sent without stamps C.O.D. and usually were sealed with red or black wax. For a fee of one penny per outgoing letter, Leigh would deliver mail to the captain of the first outbound vessel destined for the consigned port. The captains then charged a delivery fee at the next port.

Leigh ran the postal office out of his house near the foot of Spring Garden Road. Due to his many other activities, he conducted the postal business in quite a haphazard manner as witnessed by many complaints about unde-livered letters. Leigh's service, however, was partly dependent on Benjamin Franklin's monthly colonial mail packet service between New York and Falmouth, England. Storms, war and other eighteenth-century constraints kept Franklin's service irregular. Confusion exists over the extent to which Halifax was included in Franklin's packet system. Due to American republi-can tendencies, Halifax may have begun to use naval vessels to establish separate mail services from the other Atlantic colonies.

Prior to the American Revolution, mail for Quebec was often sent overland from New York, but by 1783 the need for an inland winter service by-passing the thirteen colonies was clear. Canadian deputy post-master, Hugh Finlay established in 1784 between Quebec City and Halifax the first **all-Canadian British inland postal route**. Finlay hired courier Pierre Durand at considerable expense to make the overland trip of more than a thousand kilometres (600 miles) through dense forest in Maine and New Brunswick. The exhausting round trip lasted 105 days, yet Finlay demonstrated that dispatches could reach Quebec in winter from British ports.

In travelling on foot down the St. Lawrence and across the mountains to Lake Temiscouata, down the Saint John River, across to Annapolis and on to Halifax, Durand had not truely pioneered a new mail course but instead retraced the historic route of the natives and French couriers. The old French route maintained winter communication between Quebec and Louisbourg, yet the Canadian course was considerably longer than the American route via Lake Champlain to New York, and was maintained only when tensions with the United States ran high.

Provincial Archives

The first Commissioner of Public Records or **Provincial Archivist** in British North America was Thomas Beamish Akins. In 1857, at the suggestion of Joe Howe, the Nova Scotia government appointed the Liverpool, Nova Scotia native as Commissioner of Public Records. Beamish's job involved examining, preserving, and arranging valuable public papers pertaining to the history of Nova Scotia based on Howe's credo that: "It's a wise nation that preserves its records." Working mostly out of Province House, without benefit of an archives or record storing building, Akins held the position for thirty-four years, cataloguing five hundred volumes of documents and amassing three thousand books, as well as assisting Beamish Murdoch in his classic *History of Nova Scotia*. Finally in 1931, funding for a building was obtained and the Public Archives of Nova Scotia opened on the Dalhousie University campus.

Akins also had studied law in the office of Beamish Murdoch and wrote the prize winning book *History of Halifax City*, which has been reprinted many times. In 1859, he was appointed Provincial Librarian in charge of all books and printed papers belonging to Nova Scotia. Akins' former Brunswick Street residence, Akins Cottage, is Halifax oldest home. He died in 1891.

Undersea Telegraph Cable

Engineer Frederic Gisborne laid the first **undersea telegraph cable** in North America in 1852 between Cape Tormentine, New Brunswick and Carleton Head, Prince Edward Island. Born in England, Gisborne had worked as a telegraph operator and developed an insulated wire resistant to salt water corrosion. He helped found the British North American Telegraph Company and in 1856 also laid a submarine cable between Cape Breton and Newfoundland. In 1866 that led to completion of the first transatlantic cable between Newfoundland and Ireland. Fifteen years later, the first **direct undersea cable** between England and continental North America came ashore at Canso and remained operational until 1961.

Gisborne was a brilliant innovator with boundless energy, a pioneer in Canadian science and technology. But he died in obscurity, a victim of unscrupulous partners. He also played an important role in development of Cape Breton's coalfields in the late 1800s. Citing Gisborne's historic work and recognizing the pioneering 1852 cable operation, a bronze tablet has been placed on the Provincial Building in Charlottetown.

Press Bureau and the Telegraph

Electric telegraph became the first modern method of telecommunication. Developed by American Samuel Morse in 1844 by means of electric signals moving through wires, at great speed over long distances, the telegraph proved a boom to news-gathering services. While the telegraph first came to Upper Canada, the first **Canadian telegraphic connection** of the 1,300–member Associated Press of New York was established at Saint John in 1848. Sensational European news, such as John Hamilton's 1849 attempt to shoot Queen Victoria in London's St. James Park, travelled via Cunard's transatlantic mail steamer to Halifax and couriered by pony express to Saint John and instantly telegraphed to the Associated Press office in New York.

The pony express connection involved a tremendous effort, but overseas news in New York was considered a valuable commodity. Fresh horses every nineteen kilometres (12 miles) and a new rider at the halfway point covered the 230 kilometres (144 miles) from Halifax to Victoria Beach, near Digby. Tramp steamers rushed dispatches across the Bay of Fundy to Saint John where they were transmitted by wire to New York and published the next day.

Extension of the telegraph line via Amherst to Halifax ended the pony express service. In late 1849, the Associated Press opened its first **Canadian office** in Halifax to handle European news. D.H. Craig was hired as the Press Bureau's first foreign correspondent. The first telegraph of European news from Halifax occurred on November 15, 1849 when a three thousand-word transmission reached New York a half-hour after it arrived at the Halifax waterfront.

Broadcasting and the Radio

The CBC's J. Frank Willis, made the first "on the spot" **news broadcast** in Canadain April 1936 at Moose River, Nova Scotia, during a gold mining disaster. A cave-in trapped three mining inspectors underground for nine days until draeggermen from Stellarton drilled a small tunnel to the men. Only two of the trapped men survived. Willis did ninety-nine broadcasts in ninety-six hours using a banquet table microphone in the front seat of his car "patched" directly into the telephone system. A total of fifty-eight Canadian radio stations and 650 US outlets took part in this massive hook-up that made radio history as the trapped men were rescued "live" before millions of North Americans.

Another first in Canada occurred during this mining rescue when the press agency, Wide World Syndicate, set up photographic equipment in the Lord Nelson Hotel in Halifax capable of **transmitting photographs** over telephone wires. The *New York Times* published a number of these large black and white pictures, featuring the rescued men exiting the mine shaft.

Guglielmo Marconi invented the radio and in 1901 received the first transatlantic wireless signal from England at St. John's, Newfoundland. The first **permanent radio station** in Canada was constructed the next year at Glace Bay. Marconi had been offered $80,000 by the Canadian government to establish his wireless operations on Cape Breton. The first **message** transmitted to England by Marconi: "The patient waiter never loses" made radio history, establishing a wireless radio link with Europe.

In 1907 Marconi solved his technical difficulties in wireless transmission by extending the radio waves for long distance communication and linked signals from Port Morien, Cape Breton, with his new station at Clifden, Ireland. This was the beginning of the first **commercial radio service** across the Atlantic. Marconi's small staff quickly expanded to include twenty-one operators and engineers, working around the clock, transmitting and receiving wireless messages from overseas. Later in 1919, Marconi's station at Louisbourg, Cape Breton, received the first **overseas wireless voice transmission**, this time from Letterfrack, Ireland.

Marconi had difficulty constructing his elaborate transmission stations in Cape Breton, especially when it came to acquiring and repairing technical equipment. In 1906 he established the first company in Canada to **manu-**

facture commercial radio equipment, starting a machine shop in Glace Bay. Four years later, it employed forty people but was judged too small to handle the increasing volume of orders for equipment and moved to company headquarters in Montreal.

As the North American terminus of his transatlantic electromagnetic service, Cape Breton served his three stations well until the introduction of short wave communication in 1926 rendered the coastal location obsolete. At Table Head, outside Glace Bay, a National Historic Site monument honours Guglielmo Marconi's contribution to today's global communications network.

Frederick Creed's Teleprinter

Frederick Creed, born at Mill Village, Nova Scotia, in 1871, began work as a telegraph operator but became convinced that a faster telegraphic method could be developed to communicate over long distances. While working in Peru, Creed rebuilt an old typewriter into the world's first **keyboard perforator**, allowing telegraphy tape to be automatically punched, the basis for all high-speed telegraph systems. Creed later moved from Halifax to Glasgow, and in 1901 managed to sell his first keyboard perforator to the British Post Office.

The London *Daily Mail* adopted the Creed Teleprinter system and by 1913 could transmit its entire newspaper nightly by wire. Creed then established his own business outside London, manufacturing and selling Creed equipment throughout the world. Creed's company became part of the International Telegraph and Telephone Company in 1928 while Creed himself received the Freedom of the City of London award. The original Creed teleprinter is on exhibit at the Kensington Museum, London.

Television

The first **televised broadcast** of a provincial legislature in Canada occurred in the Nova Scotia Legislative Assembly, Halifax, March 22 1971. Television equipment stationed in the public galleries taped portions of the legislature proceeding which were re-broadcast on local TV stations. As part of the three week trial period, local radio stations also received live sound from the Hansard sound system.

Arts

"They make . . . works worthy of admiration, with the hairs of porcupine, coloured with red, black, white, and blue . . ., so lively that ours seem in nothing to be comparable to them." — Marc Lescarbot, commenting in his 1609 *History of New France* on his discovery of Mi'kmaq quillwork at Port Royal.

Early Maritime Theatre

Historian and lawyer Marc Lescarbot wrote and produced the first **European theatre** presentation in North America, *Le Théâtre de Neptune en la Nouvelle-France*, in 1606 at Port Royal. Performed on several small boats by settlers as well as Mi'kmaq, the Theatre of Neptune greeted Baron Poutrincourt's return to Port Royal and depicted the god Neptune welcoming the travellers to Acadia. Written in the French tradition of a reception or masque, the play included both music and singing during the "Great God Neptune" piece as well as dialogue incorporating Mi'kmaq roles and words. Lescarbot later included the play in his 1609 published collection, *Les Muses de la Nouvelle-France*.

Samuel de Champlain organized the first entertainment or **social club** in North America at Port Royal during the winter of 1606. Attempting to boost settler morale after a miserable experience the previous winter, Champlain formed the Order of Good Cheer. Members took turns as steward of an evening feast, gathering and preparing the meal as well as entertaining the native guests, often including Mi'kmaq chief Membertou. Each member would try to outdo the previous merry making with special food, speeches, plays and other literary creations.

English-language drama in British North America seems to have begun in Halifax where the dramatic arts flourished in the latter half of the

46

eighteenth century under the patronage of the British army and naval officers, including Prince Edward.

The American Company of Comedians, was the first **professional company of actors** to establish residency in Canada. Known to have performed a tragedy, *Jane Shore*, and a farce called *The Virgin Unmask'D or, an old man taught wisdom*, on September 2, 1768, the company's performances were likely held at the Pontac Coffee House & Inn at the corner of Duke and Water streets. The Inn's large assembly room served as the setting for a number of early Halifax events, including General Wolfe's farewell dinner in 1758 held prior to his departure for the siege of Louisbourg.

The earliest known **theatre** in Canada, The Grand Theatre, opened in Halifax on Argyle Street in 1789, three years before a theatre appeared in Boston and fifteen years before one began in Montreal. Puritan sentiment had prevented theatres from being constructed throughout New England, but Halifax's new theatre enjoyed considerable popular success with the first plays performed being *The Merchant of Venice* and *The Citizen*. Popular farces were all the rage, often acted by young British military officers.

Written and performed in Halifax in 1774, the first **original English Canadian play** was a romantic comedy in three acts, entitled *Acadius; or, Love in a Calm*. Advertised in the *Nova Scotia Gazette* as being performed for the benefit of "late sufferers of Fire," *Acadius* most likely was also staged at the Pontac Inn.

Dramatic performances in New Brunswick began in 1789 at the Mallard House on King Street in Saint John where the first **provincial Legislative Assembly** met in 1786 and city council continued to meet until 1797. The Mallard House had also been known as the scene of the first political riot in Canada in 1785. Plays performed in the Long Room were *The Busy Body* and *Who's The Dupe?* New Brunswick's first theatrical evening was advertised in the *Royal Gazette* with proceeds of three shillings each going to public charity and no ticket sales at the door. The dramatic evening was well attended by the Loyalist establishment of Saint John as well as by Colonel Edward Winslow who wrote of the performance, "Nonsense never fails to please if it is civil." Winslow had made a special effort to attend travelling on the frozen Saint John River from his home at Kingsclear, above Fredericton.

Arts Organization

The Halifax Chess, Pencil and Brush Club became Canada's first known **organization of artists** in 1787. Formed as a social club but also to encourage the colonial society's patronage of the arts, the association often attempted to extend its influence beyond artistic matters to address political questions of the day. The club met for years at the Pontac Inn and its first president was the Honourable Richard Bulkeley. He became the colony's pre-eminent civil servant, often called the Father of Nova Scotia. Bulkeley had arrived with Cornwallis during the founding of Halifax and over a period of fifty-nine years served thirteen governors, from Cornwallis to Wentworth, in numerous senior positions.

Wealthy from his Irish inheritance, Bulkeley entertained lavishly at his stone mansion, the Carleton House, now part of the old Carleton Hotel complex opposite St. Paul's Church. He died in 1800, the last surviving member of the colonists who had established Halifax in 1749. Bulkeley was buried in St Paul's, a church he helped build, after one of the largest funerals ever recorded in Halifax. His coat of arms is displayed in the west gallery of the church. Without Bulkeley as its president, membership in the arts club waned and the organization folded in 1817.

Art Exhibition

A **public exhibition of art**, the first known in British North America, was held at Halifax's Dalhousie College in May of 1830. Organized by Dalhousie's first art instructor, American William H. Jones, and under the patronage of Dalhousie president Michael Wallace and Admiral Sir Charles Ogle, the exhibition included works by students as well as local artists, such as the celebrated Halifax painter and photographer William Valentine.

Modelled after a similar public show held in Boston, the exhibition revealed its New England influence by including a Copley canvas as well as paintings seized as prize booty from American ships during the War of 1812. One report of Canada's earliest public art show cites native art as also on display and, if so, the 1830 exhibit would have been the first exhibition by native artists in Canada. Located opposite St. Paul's Church on the Grand Parade, Dalhousie remained a central point in Halifax's downtown cultural life until its move to the city's south end in the late 1800s.

Milestones in Literary Publishing

The first Canadian **periodical** was *The Nova Scotia Magazine And Comprehensive Review Of Literature, Politics, And News,* published in 1789 in Halifax. Edited by the New York Loyalist, Dr. William Cochran, principal of the Halifax Grammar School and later the first principal of King's College at Windsor, the eighty-page monthly was printed by Joe Howe's father, John Howe. The literary magazine contained anecdotes, selected articles, original poetry and local news, as well as items clipped from the American and British presses. Howe's journal may have been too ambitious for the period and also too expensive at four dollars per year. With only 223 subscribers the first year, the magazine folded after three years.

The first **novel** by a Canadian to be published in Canada was written by Fredericton author, Julia Beckwith Hart. Her two-volume novel, *St. Ursula's Convent; or, The Nun of Canada,* was written when she was seventeen and published ten years later in 1824 by Kingston, Ontario, newspaper publisher Hugh C. Thompson. The suspense-filled novel is set in a French-Canadian world of the gothic imagination. The two volumes were handsomely bound in green with gold lettering, although only 165 copies are thought to have been issued. One of the few women writers of the period, Hart also wrote two more novels, including *Tonnewonte; or, The Adopted Son of America,* which was published in the United States.

The **Canadian author** to first achieve international recognition was Thomas Chandler Haliburton with his work *The Clockmaker; or the Saying and Doing of Sam Slick of Slickville.* Published by Joe Howe, initially in instalments in the *Novascotian,* and then in book form in 1836, *The Clockmaker* appeared in over eighty editions worldwide. Haliburton's other writings were popular but *The Clockmaker,* featuring the wisecracking clockmaker Sam Slick and his social satire, firmly established the Windsor judge and politician's literary reputation. Haliburton is often considered the first American humorist with his literary creation, the Yankee Sam Slick, while Thomas McCulloch's *Letters of Mephibosheth* is considered the first work of **Canadian humour.** McCulloch's writing first appeared in the *Acadian Recorder* at Halifax between 1821-1823. McCulloch also founded the Pictou Academy and in 1818 became the first president of Dalhousie University.

The earliest known **poems** to have been printed in Canada were Henry Alline's *Hymns and Spiritual Songs*. A first edition was printed in Halifax in 1780 by Anthony Henry as a small twenty-four page pamphlet containing twenty-two of his composed hymns and songs. Alline later expanded the work and published the fuller version in Boston, perhaps because he found the garrison town of Halifax "a land of darkness." He did however, use Henry's services to print two additional works on theology, *Two Mites* (1781) and *The Anti-Traditional* (1783).

The first **native-born, English-speaking poet** in Canada was Oliver Goldsmith. Born in St. Andrews in 1794, Goldsmith grew up in Annapolis Royal and wrote his famous poem, *The Rising Village*, during his stay in Halifax. It was published in London in 1825 and again in Canada ten years later by Saint John bookseller-publisher, John McMillan. Influenced by his Irish great-uncle's *The Deserted Village*, which portrayed the decline of the rural life in Europe, Goldsmith describes the opposite situation in the New World, the rise of the rural village.

While not considered a literary masterpiece, *The Rising Village* was the first **book-length poem** published by an English-Canadian and did contribute to the embryonic Canadian literature of the period. A simple and direct account of the emerging Maritime community life, Goldsmith's poem was written in heroic couplets and became something of a nineteenth-century literary anthem. Goldsmith's autobiography was discovered in Annapolis Royal in 1939 by Father Wilfred Myatt, who edited and published the work four years later through the Ryerson Press.

Considered the first truly **Canadian poet**, with his 1880 book, *Orion, And Other Poems*, Charles G.D. Roberts is credited with establishing Canada's first **national literary movement**. A founding member of the Poets of Confederation, Roberts is generally regarded as the first English-speaking Canadian poet to bring a new national spirit to Canadian poetry, inspired by the Canadian landscape itself, as well as the aspirations of the new nation.

Based in Fredericton, Roberts lived and worked throughout the Maritimes and abroad. With his achievements of poetic verse, Roberts inspired a number of notable poets, including his cousin, Bliss Carman, Francis Joseph Sherman, and Archibald Lampman.

The first Canadian **poet to be knighted**, Roberts was regarded as one of Canada's leading scholars at the time of his death in 1943. A memorial cairn, entitled The Poet's Corner of Canada, has been erected on the grounds of the University of New Brunswick campus in Fredericton and is dedicated to the memory of these Confederation poets. Roberts was much more than a poet and is often considered the father of Canadian literature, writing hundreds of short stories, as well as novels, essays, and articles during his distinguished literary career. He shares with Ernest Thompson Seton credit for establishing the **Canadian animal story** as a popular literary form, pioneering the concept of telling an unsentimental story from the animal's point of view.

The Canadian **children's writer** to first achieve international status was Nova Scotian author Margaret Saunders with her autobiography of an abused dog, *Beautiful Joe*. Written in 1894 and first published outside Canada by the American Humane Society, the book was translated into more than twenty languages and is often cited as the first Canadian written **book to sell over a million copies**. Saunders wrote many animal stories for children and travelled widely, conducting her illustrated lectures on the humane treatment of animals. Her Carleton Street home in Halifax contained an aviary and injured birds were often brought there by the children of Halifax.

While Margaret Saunders may have been the first major Canadian children's author, her popularity waned in the latter stages of the twentieth century. Consequently, Lucy Maud Montgomery can be considered the first Canadian **children's author** to achieve more lasting international recognition. *Anne of Green Gables* was published in 1908 and Montgomery's red-headed heroine, Anne Shirley, is more popular today, almost ninety years later, than when she first appeared in print. Several Anne sequels were written and, while all were well received, none achieved the popularity of the original work.

Antonine Maillet from Bouctouche, New Brunswick became the first North American to win the most important literary prize in the French-speaking world, the **Prix Goncourt**, for her 1979 novel, *Pélagie-la-Charrette*. The Acadian writer had previously won international recognition with her 1971 novel *La Sagouine*, depicting the hardships and strength of the Acadian culture. Through Pélagie, Maillet symbolizes the determination of the Acadian people as Pélagie spends ten years trying to return to Acadia with her cart and cow, after being deported to the southern states. Maillet's influence in contemporary Acadian culture coincides with the current Acadian cultural revival.

The study of **Canadian literature** in English may well have first occurred at the University of Guelph (Macdonald Institute) in 1906-07, but Acadia University claims to have introduced a course specify devoted to Canadian literature in 1915, taught by John Daniel Logan.

First Public Museum

With the assistance of Abraham Gesner, the inventor of kerosene, the first **public museum** in Canada was opened in 1842 in Saint John. Appointed the Provincial Geologist for New Brunswick in 1837, Gesner and his family moved to McNab's Hill in Saint John. Within five years, Gesner had collected over two thousand unusual items from the Maritimes, including animal and bird fossils, minerals and plants, even two human skulls. All appeared in a printed catalogue listing 2,173 items. Gesner began inviting the public to view his collection on display in his home.

Heavily in debt and unable to remain in Saint John, Gesner gave his collection to his creditors who donated the items to the local Mechanics Institute. The institute, which became an important educational centre for workers, had erected a building on Carleton Street in 1840 and on April 5, 1842, with Gesner in attendance, opened a room centred around his collection called the Museum of Natural History. Public exhibits were organized and eventually, through the efforts of William Ganong and others, the collection was merged with the artifacts of the Natural History Society of New Brunswick to form the Provincial Museum of New Brunswick.

Today Gesner's original collection is an important part of the New Brunswick Museum's impressive holdings, which include the Webster and Ganong collections. In addition to New Brunswick's natural history, the decorative arts as well as the province's marine history are important features of the museum's current collection.

Indoor Studio and Outdoor Photography

The birth of photography is usually credited to L. Daguerre of Paris, who in 1839 developed the process of producing an image on a silver-covered copper plate. Daguerreotype was originally called sun painting since half-hour exposures in strong sunlight were not uncommon. The new art quickly became popular and in 1841, Halifax portrait painter William Valentine left Boston, stopping in Saint John to demonstrate the new process. He returned to Halifax in January of 1842 to become the first Canadian to begin a **photographic studio** in British North America.

A number of Americans had earlier set up temporary Daguerreotype shops in Quebec, but Valentine can be claimed as the first permanent daguerreotypist to appear in the British colonies. Valentine may well have also produced the first **known photograph** in Canada. There is considerable speculation that Valentine was the "friend" cited in the Halifax *Colonial Pearl*'s article of June, 1839, claiming that "one of our friends who read the article (an earlier item describing the Daguerreotype process) has since formed several photogenic pictures with ease and success."

This new art was accessible to people unable to afford an oil portrait and Valentine is also thought to have been the first to introduce this photographic technique to Newfoundland and Prince Edward Island. John Clow, who worked with Valentine, is known to have opened the first portrait studio in Saint John around the same time. Few identified images have survived the period but this new process of capturing pictures with a memory, quickly became one of the most sought after skills in Canada.

George T. Taylor of Fredericton is considered the pioneer of **nature photography**. Born in 1838 on Brunswick Street in Fredericton, Taylor began working for Fredericton's first photographer David Lawrence in 1856. He reportedly acquired a lens and constructed his first wooden camera the same year. He travelled with Maliseet guides into the wilds of New Brunswick with heavy photographic supplies and developing equipment, producing some of the earliest known wilderness photographs.

Taylor's outdoor photos reveal some of the most remote corners of New Brunswick and are indeed marvellous images considering the huge and bulky equipment he dragged into the bush by canoe and sled. The photos were developed using the wet-plate development process pioneered by Frederick

George Taylor's Maliseet guide in the New Brunswick wilderness about 1862. Canada's first nature photographer always travelled with his extensive photographic euipment. (New Brunswick Public Archives)

Archer. In 1874 a new dry-plate process was introduced that George Eastman successfully mass-produced. Taylor was known to have further adopted and simplified this picture developing technique and also is said to have invented the printing of photographic blueprints. This is not surprising since he also built or assembled all his cameras and processing equipment. Many of Taylor's photographs appeared in Canada's first national news magazine, the *Canadian Illustrated News*, which began publishing in 1869.

By 1900, photography was no longer the exciting, new picture-making process that had intrigued the public for sixty years. As the Eastman company began mass producing cameras, Taylor stopped his photographic work in 1906, returning to his youthful passion of painting. He died in 1913. Through the efforts of Lord Beaverbrook, many of Taylor's large glass plates are preserved at the New Brunswick Archives in Fredericton. The Archives' official opening in 1968 was marked by an exhibition of photographs, paintings and memorabilia of George Taylor.

Oldest Art Gallery

The oldest commercial **art gallery** in Canada is Zwicker's Gallery, established in 1886 in Halifax's north end and currently located on Doyle Street. The gallery was started by Judson A. Zwicker as an art supply framing shop, selling prints and reproductions to British military officers.

Beginning in the 1930s, Judson Zwicker's son LeRoy began a small gallery at the rear of the shop while still a student at the Nova Scotia College of Art. During the Depression, LeRoy painted and also worked as a retail manager at Moirs, the chocolate company. In 1938, he married a Yarmouth County painter who also taught at the art college. Together LeRoy and Marguerite Zwicker ran Halifax's only commercial art gallery and supported the visual arts in Nova Scotia, promoting local and Canadian artists.

Under their ownership, Zwicker's Gallery became one of the best-known galleries in Canada, specializing in Canadian as well as Maritime art, including watercolours. LeRoy Zwicker also helped found the art magazine, *Maritime Art*, later known as *Arts Canada*. In recognition of their life's work promoting Maritime visual arts, a LeRoy and Marguerite Zwicker Gallery has been established as part of the Art Gallery of Nova Scotia.

Singing Choir

The first **coal miner singing choir** in North America was formed in Glace Bay in 1966 as part of Cape Breton's contribution to Canada's 1967 Centennial celebration. All members of The Men of The Deeps choir are either miners or retired miners and perform in miner's working clothes, including helmets with headlamps. They have recorded albums and sang worldwide for over twenty-five years, often appearing with Anne Murray and Rita MacNeil. Largely through the efforts of Nina Cohen, who had earlier founded the Miner's Folk Society, and musical director Jack O'Donnell, the chorus has developed into a national treasure featuring the musical tradition from the Cape Breton coal mines.

Evangeline, the Film

While the first film in Canada was made in Manitoba, *Evangeline*, made in Halifax in 1913 by the Canadian Bioscope Company, was the first dramatic feature length, **motion picture**, made in Canada. Based on Longfellow's poem about the 1755 expulsion of the Acadians, the film's narrative closely follows the poem's story.

Many of the scenes were shot in authentic locations throughout the Annapolis Valley. The picture was successful, both critically and at the box office. A favourable review in the New York film journal, *The Moving Picture World*, claimed that "Good judgement has been displayed in the making of this five-part subject — good picture judgement. The picture is well acted."

Staged and directed by experienced screen actors E. P. Sullivan and W. H. Cavanaugh, the film featured American actors in the leading roles Laura Lyman as Evangeline and John F. Carleton as Gabriel. The British-owned company produced another six films, both dramas and comedies, over the next few years but could not repeat the success of *Evangeline*. By 1915, the Bioscope film company had stopped making movies.

The first **motion pictures screened** in the Maritimes were arranged by Edwin Porter, who also performed a vaudeville act with the touring company, Wormwood's Dog and Monkey Show, the name given a contemporary Halifax theatre.

Transportation

"Ladies and gentlemen, last trip I astonished the world with the sailing of this ship. This trip I intend to astonish God Almighty!" Captain Bully Forbes aboard the *Marco Polo* on its second voyage to Australia. — Frederick William Wallace, *Wooden Ships And Iron Men*.

Canoe and the Snowshoe

When Europeans arrived in northeastern North America, Mi'kmaq and Maliseet forms of transportation so impressed them, they immediately adopted the **canoe** and **snowshoe**. Like the snowshoe, North American Indians invented the birchbark canoe. Distinctively fashioned by the Mi'kmaq, its centre sides curved upward in order to remain stable in open water. White birchbark sown together with split spruce root and caulked with spruce gum, produced an excellent, lightweight vehicle for use along Maritime rivers, lakes, and coastal waters. Inland, especially around the Saint John River where the best white birch grew, the Maliseet river canoes reached the height of craftsmanship in both beauty and function.

In winter, the snowshoe was equally impressive in transporting people over the frozen landscape. Using an oval-shaped frame of ash, the Mi'kmaq wove rawhide, the uncured skin of moose or caribou, in order to support a heavy load over snow. Often a wooden toboggan or sled was pulled as well, with loads as heavy as two hundred kilograms (440 pounds), often transported over long distances.

Wooden Ships and Shipbuilding

In addition to the canoe, Maritime aboriginals also built **wooden frame boats** covered with animal hides. The first **European-built boat** in North America is reported to have been constructed at Port Royal in 1606 by François Gravé du Pont. Two small vessels were built, a barque and a shallop, after promised supply ships did not arrive in time to transport settlers to Cape Breton.

The golden age of trade for the Maritime Provinces is usually considered to have been between 1830-1890, the era of the square-rigged merchant ships. British North American windjammers, often built in small coastal villages throughout the Maritimes, captured a large share of the world's merchant trade.

The *William D. Lawrence*, built in 1874 at Maitland, Nova Scotia, was the largest Maritime and third largest Canadian built, fully rigged wooden sailing vessel. Lloyd's registered the *Lawrence* at 2,230 metric tons (2,459 tons), seventy-three metric tons (80 tons), heavier than the next largest Maritime vessel, *Morning Light*, built at Saint John in 1855.

The largest **clipper ship** ever built, the four-masted barque *Great Republic*, registered 5,443 metric tons (6,000 tons) and was constructed in 1853 at East Boston by a Jordan Falls, Nova Scotia shipbuilder, Donald McKay. McKay, perhaps the most famous pioneer builder of square-rigged merchant ships, built over seventy wooden vessels at his Massachusetts shipyard before turning to iron ships in the 1860s. McKay made many improvements to the clipper ship design, culminating in one of the fastest afloat, the *Flying Cloud* which set a New York to San Francisco record that has never been surpassed. It wrecked in 1874 on a mud bank in Saint John harbour.

The *Marco Polo*, New Brunswick's most famous clipper, became the **fastest ship** in the world after establishing a world record from Liverpool, England, to Australia and back, in under six months. Launched in 1851, at Marsh Creek, Saint John, the *Marco Polo* was a large cargo ship with a registered metric tonnage of 1,474 (1,625 tons). Built by James Smith, the ship was not a true clipper but combined the underwater sharpness of a clipper with the midship bulk of a cargo carrier.

Built in Saint John in 1851, the *Marco Polo* set new sailing records to Australia. (Artist John Johnson, oil on canvas, New Brunswick Museum, Saint John, N.B.)

The captain, "Bully" Forbes, made good on his boast of out and back to Australia in less than 180 days, via Cape Horn. He astonished the shipping world when the round trip was accomplished in five months, twenty-one days. For several days at sea, the *Marco Polo* logged over 576 kilometres (360 miles) per day, reaching cruising speeds of seventeen knots, a rare occurrence for such a huge cargo ship, carrying 930 emigrants and a crew of sixty.

One explanation for the *Marco Polo*'s speed despite its ordinary appearance has to do with an accident during launching. She fell over on her side, producing an altered keel. The concave keel may have mysteriously given her freak speed since other ships with her dimensions could not duplicate her sailing records. With the *Marco Polo*, Saint John's shipbuilding reputation was firmly established throughout the shipping world. British shipowners began placing orders with New Brunswick shipbuilders, especially the celebrated James Smith. Lying offshore at Cavendish, Prince Edward Island, the *Marco Polo* was caught in a gale in 1883 and went down. A wooden carved figurehead from the vessel was later retrieved and now forms part of the New Brunswick Museum's Marine Gallery.

The timber trade, especially the shipment of lumber to Britain, created the strongest and most profitable shipbuilding period in British North America. The largest shipment of lumber received from North America at England's great nineteenth-century seaport, Liverpool,was 484,403 metres (1,589,250 feet), of **deals lumber** from the Miramichi-Kent County area of New Brunswick. The ship *Chinchas*, built in 1858 by the Holderness and Mcleod yard in Kent County, hauled the cargo. A deal became the nineteenth-century standard for measuring lumber, usually softwood, of at least twenty-three centimetres (9 inches) wide and eight centimetres (3 inches) thick. The first recorded shipment of hand-cut deals from the Maritimes left Saint John for Cork, Ireland, in 1822.

Lumberman and farmers used the **Saint John River woodboat**, peculiar to the geographical requirements of the lower Saint John River Valley, primarily as a wood carrier. As river cargo carriers, the woodboats were unequaled until about the time of Confederation. The woodboat was distinguished from a schooner by the absence of a bowsprit and headsail. A stub-nosed vessel with a flat bottom and bilge keel, to permit it to stand upright when left dry by the ebb of the huge Bay of Fundy tides, the woodboat began to appear around the Grand Lake and Long Reach area, in the late eighteenth century.

Brought to New Brunswick by the Loyalists and adapted to meet local conditions, the woodboat was indeed unique to the region. Weighing under ninety-one metric tons (100 tons), the vessel seems to have been developed from traditional New England vessels, including the Chebacco and the Dogbody, and began to be called a woodboat about 1812. Besides timber, these marine workhorses often transported coal, hay, passengers, as well as general cargo and were crucial to the early development of New Brunswick. The last boat was built in 1917 and the last of these vessels to haul cargo reportedly broke up at Saint John in 1930. It is estimated that about five hundred vessels in total were built.

The **Tancook Whaler**, a fine fore-and-aft schooner-rigged fishing vessel, first appeared around Mahone Bay, between 1860 and 1870. The first schooner seems to have been built at Lunenburg but the vessel was pioneered by the Stevens, Masons, and Langilles whaler builders, chiefly Amos Stevens and Alfred Langille, on Big Tancook Island at the mouth of Mahone Bay.

Built between eight and sixteen meters (25 to 50 feet) in length, the whaler had a unique hull, with a length to beam ratio of four to one, allowing for efficient rowing but when fitted with ballast and cargo, was also able to run under sail. This schooner-rigged vessel served the island people of Mahone Bay well and was quite seaworthy, ideal for the rough seas and strong winds of the Atlantic coast. By World War I, few vessels were still being built and the Tancook whaler as a working schooner all but disappeared by 1940.

About the same time, the common dory reached its peak of popularity as the Grand Bank trawl fishery reached its pinnacle. Perfect for the trawl fishing industry, the flat-bottomed dories began to be successfully mass-produced in 1887 when Shelburne dory builder Issac Crowell started to make dory knees by breaking with tradition and joining two straight pieces of wood. Previously all dory knee braces had been made from rare, naturally curved or crooked wood and Crowell's patent **dory clip** allowed for the cheap yet durable dories to be produced by the thousands. Shelburne became one of the best known centres for dory construction with numerous dory shops churning out thousands of small vessels for the entire East Coast fishery. One famous Shelburne boat builder, Sidney Mahaney, constructed dories in his shop for almost eighty years.

The **Cape Island Boat** was developed by shipbuilder Ephram Atkinson on Cape Sable Island, at Clark's Harbour, about 1900. Atkinson realized that the emerging gasoline engines would be unsuitable for fitting into the existing inshore sailing vessels. The unique aspect of Atkinson's Cape Islander was its hull design which allowed for an engine and fuel, but gave the vessel good stability to power through the open water, carrying a load of fish. The small boat first pioneered by Atkinson in 1907 has now become the standard design for small working boats in the North Atlantic, especially in the lobster industry. As a gasoline-powered fishing craft, drawing little water yet highly stable, the Cape Island boat allowed fisherman to more efficiently exploit the marine resources, and at the same time made their life at sea somewhat easier.

Canada's First Shipwreck

The earliest known **shipwreck** in waters of what is today part of Canada occurred in 1583 at Sable Island, off Nova Scotia, when Sir Humphrey Gilbert's 108 metric ton (120 ton) ship the *Delight*, went down. Gilbert himself was aboard another ship the *Squirrel*. He escaped danger off Sable only to perish while returning to England in heavy seas north of the Azores.

A highly ambitious Elizabethan figure, Gilbert had Queen Elizabeth I's blessing for his expedition to establish a settlement in North America, yet Gilbert's seamanship was not sufficient to lead such a voyage of exploration. An eyewitness account left by Captain Edward Hayes, who was aboard the only ship to return to England, the *Golden Hind*, made it clear Gilbert's decision to approach Sable at night during a storm sealed the expedition's fate.

Sixteen men survived the shipwreck off Sable Island and fourteen, including their chief navigator Richard Clarke, reached Newfoundland after seven days adrift in a lifeboat equipped with a single oar. Since then more than five hundred ships have gone aground on this island of sand known as the Graveyard of the Atlantic.

Maritime Lighthouses

The first **lighthouse** in Canada beamed its cod-liver oil burning light out to mariners in 1734 from the eastern side of Louisbourg harbour. The wooden casing of the lantern caught fire two years later and the lantern room was rebuilt in fireproof brick and lead, becoming the only **fireproof building** in North America. The oil was deemed too hot by the French authorities and a mixture of coal and wood was introduced. Light from the eighteen-metre (60 foot) tower reportedly could be seen twenty-nine kilometres (18 miles) out to sea. The British destroyed the tower while capturing the Fortress of Louisbourg in 1758 but rebuilt it in 1824.

The **oldest existing lighthouse** in Canada stands on Sambro Island at the outer approaches to Halifax harbour. Its first lightkeeper was Captain Joseph Rous and the light, fuelled by sperm whale oil, broke through the darkness in 1760 after being built with funds raised from a lottery and taxes on liquor. The first optical lens at Sambro was manufactured in Paris and was installed in 1906. It is now on display at the Maritime Museum of the Atlantic in Halifax.

Lighthouses began by using open fires of wood and coal, changed to cod, whale, and vegetable oils, and, after Abraham Gesner discovered kerosene in 1846, switched to this coal oil, and finally to petroleum and electrical lamps. Gesner first experimented with his gas fuel in 1851 on McNabs Island in Halifax harbour and gradually was able to convince the Canadian Lighthouse Commission to try his invention.

New Brunswick's first **lighthouse** was erected in 1791 on Partridge Island in Saint John harbour. In 1859 the world's first steam fog horn became operational based on a design by Saint John inventor, Robert Foulis.The island also served as a signal station, New Brunswick's first **radio station**, coast guard base, military battery, as well as a quarantine station for thousands of immigrants. Twice designated a National Historic Site, Partridge Island today is still a coast guard base and open for summer tours.

The first **lifesaving station** in Canada was established in 1823 at Seal Island, Nova Scotia, when Mary Crowell Hichens and her husband moved to the island to assist shipwrecked sailors. Less than one quarter the size of Sable Island, Seal Island almost rivalled Sable in the number of shipwrecks off its shoals. Situated twenty-four kilometres (15 miles) west of Cape Sable Island near the entrance to the Bay of Fundy, the island had been uninhabited. Many shipwrecked victims perished in the bitter cold Atlantic winds after reaching the island. No lives were lost near the island after 1823. Richard Hichens became the island's first lighthouse keeper in 1831 when the provinces of Nova Scotia and New Brunswick jointly built a lighthouse at the island's southern end.

Ferry Shuttle Service

The first regular saltwater **ferry service** in North America began in 1752 between Halifax and Dartmouth as regular passage across the harbour became necessary for the growing communities. George Gerrish had established a wind-driven sawmill at Dartmouth the same year and settlers were beginning to build homes along the harbour. John Conner was granted a three-year charter to run two boats regularly between sunrise and sunset at sixpence a trip. Baggage was transported at no additional charge. Conner's original boats were essentially rowboats with a single sail. Only one round trip was made on Sundays in order to allow Dartmouth citizens to attend church services in Halifax.

John Conner died suddenly in 1754 and his tombstone is the oldest in Halifax's first **burial grounds**, the Old Burying Ground on Barrington Street. Yet ferry service continued uninterrupted. For almost 250 years, dozens of vessels have continued to provide constant shuttle service for passengers between the shores of Halifax harbour.

Atlantic Neptune

While most white explorers had charts and maps, the first systematic **survey** of the eastern North American coastline was undertaken by Joseph Frederick DesBarres between 1764 and 1773. DesBarres was a unique and colourful figure in Maritime history. A Swiss Huguenot, DesBarres was an assistant engineer during the final seige of Louisbourg and charted the St. Lawrence River for James Wolfe. Commissioned by the British government to accurately chart the coast and harbours of the east coast, DesBarres spent almost ten years with twenty or more workers and seven assistants, mapping what was then known as the Nova Scotia coast.

DesBarres' precise hydrographic methods and artistic genius resulted in a magnificent collection of charts and paintings measuring fifty-eight by eighty-six centimetres (23 by 34 inches). Called *The Atlantic Neptune*, the work became the standard navigational aide for mariners for the next fifty years. A landmark in Canadian cartographic work, *The Atlantic Neptune* was the first great **atlas** of views and charts produced about North America. It charted the Atlantic coast from the Gulf of St. Lawrence south to Chesapeake Bay.

DesBarres had worked relentlessly for years to produce his survey for the Royal Navy, almost drowning off Sable Island, and felt he had received less than adequate compensation for his work. In 1784 he was appointed the first **lieutenant governor** of Cape Breton and laid out the town of Sydney as the capital of the new colony. He also became lieutenant governor of Prince Edward Island in 1804 but in both cases was too quarrelsome to be a successful governor. He died at Halifax at age 102, reputed to have celebrated his hundredth birthday by dancing on top of a table, and was buried beneath St. George's Church.

Mr. Cunard's Steam Ships

The first vessel to complete the **transatlantic crossing** wholly under steam was the paddle steamer *Royal William*, which left Pictou on August 18, 1833, and arrived in England twenty days later. Built by the Quebec and Halifax Steam Navigation Company, whose ownership group included entrepreneur Samuel Cunard, the *Royal William* began its career steaming between Quebec and Halifax but due to a cholera outbreak on board was quarantined outside Quebec and seized for outstanding debt. Sent to England to be sold, the steamer made history by crossing the Atlantic without assistance from sail, powered by coal from Pictou County's Albion Mines.

Samuel Cunard was one of the first Maritimers to establish a successful international company when, at Joe Howe's suggestion, he founded the British and North America Royal Mail Steam Packet Company, establishing the first regular **steamer mail service** between England, Halifax, and Boston. In 1840 the first mail service arrived at Halifax on board the steam ship *Britannia*, and two days later, it docked in Boston. Cunard's shipping line later became one of the world's great passenger lines with regular service aboard the *Queen Mary* and *Queen Elizabeth*.

Marine Screw Propeller

John Patch of Yarmouth was a sea captain as well as an inventor, and around 1833 devised the notion of propelling ships by means of a **screw propeller**. During the winter of 1833, Patch worked secretly on his invention at Kelly's Cove, near Yarmouth. The following summer before a crowd in Yarmouth harbour, he experimented with a wooden device in a small boat, a crude propeller model controlled by two men standing on deck, turning a hand-crank with wooden gears. The citizens of Yarmouth were astounded to see the boat move forward without sail or oar.

In 1834, he installed a similar screw propulsion system on the schooner *Royal George* with the blessing of Captain Silas C. Kelley. Outside Saint John harbour, Patch and Captain Kelly were able to turn the machinery by a crank and thrust the vessel through the calm Bay of Fundy waters, astonishing those who watched. Patch attempted to have his device patented in the United States but seems to have been unsuccessful, yet screw propellers became one of the key advances for marine steam power in the 1840s by allowing ships to dispense with the huge and inefficient paddle wheels.

One story claims that Patch's invention was stolen by insiders at the Washington patent office, a claim that could be possible since a period of corruption within the United States' patent office did exist about this time. Despite local efforts to recognize his work, including a local petition to the Nova Scotia Legislature, John Patch died penniless, an inmate of the Yarmouth poorhouse. While ownership is at best unclear, since screw propellers may have also been invented during this period in Europe, John Patch was at least the co-inventor of this important advance in marine transportation.

Compound Steam Engine

Benjamin Franklin Tibbets began his early working career in Woodstock and Fredericton as a watchmaker's apprentice. Displaying a natural talent for machinery and intricate gadgets, Tibbets became fascinated with the new steam power and its potential for marine transportation. After working in New England, Tibbets returned to Fredericton in 1845 and convinced Fredericton businessman Thomas Pickard to finance construction of a river steamboat, the *Reindeer*, propelled by Tibbets' invention, the first **compound marine steam engine** in Canada.

Prior to the *Reindeer*, steamboats were driven by either low-pressure or high-pressure engines that were largely inefficient. Tibbet's stroke of genius was the construction of a single engine, capable of utilizing steam under both pressures. Both the *Reindeer* and its two-cylinder, fifty horsepower engine were constructed at a Fredericton shipyard using local supplies, although the engine's cast iron was forged in Saint John. Throughout the Saint John River, new cruising records were set, including a voyage between Saint John and Fredericton in five hours and five minutes. Tibbets and his brother built a second vessel, the *Benjamin Franklin*, complete with a compound engine and established a steamer service between Saint John and Grand Lake.

Benjamin Tibbets died tragically at age thirty-five of tuberculosis at his father's Saint John River home. Reports that his steamer *Benjamin Franklin* burned while he lay dying are wrong, since the vessel is known to have been destroyed two years later in the upper end of Grand Lake. His grave at Scotchtown bears a monument, citing his compound engine as sparking a revolution in marine engineering, preceding European use by at least three years. Although Tibbets secured patents in New Brunswick and Lower Canada, he was unsuccessful in attempts to patent his invention in the United States. His idea was not new, only its use in marine engines was novel.

Benjamin Tibbets' remarkable achievement was to produce a practical and economical compound steam engine that helped establish the reliability and efficiency of the emerging steam-powered engines during the 1840s. By the close of the nineteenth century, steam ships had become the supreme mode of marine transportation, challenging sailing ships for domination of the sea lanes. As late as 1930, Tibbets' original double-expansion engine was reported still in storage outside Saint John. Within the city, a second monument erected by the Historic Sites and Monuments Board of Canada was installed to honour Benjamin Tibbets' achievement.

Robert Foulis' Fog Horn

Robert Foulis invented the **steam fog horn** around 1854 and five years later the world's first steam fog device was installed on Partridge Island in Saint John harbour. Foulis was born in Scotland and immigrated to North America. Shipwrecked on Nova Scotia's coast, he earned a living in Halifax as a portrait painter before moving to Saint John in 1822 to work as an civil engineer.

A Victorian inventor and entrepreneur with wide interests, Foulis had studied surgery at the University of Glasgow but became more interested in artistic pursuits. He established New Brunswick's first **iron foundry**, surveyed the Saint John River above Fredericton for steam navigation, and founded a school of arts, as well as a Mechanics' Institute in Saint John. Foulis' public lectures on chemistry were always filled to capacity.

But Foulis' outstanding contribution to marine navigation was his steam fog horn that sounded automatically in foggy weather, providing mariners with pinpoint accuracy in locating nearby land. He reportedly conceived the notion while experiencing first-hand the helplessness of a person out on the water in a thick fog. The fog alarm automatically permitted compressed steam to escape at given intervals through a large horn able to carry sound many miles across the water. Apparently Foulis decided to establish his fog horn in the key of G after hearing the note from a piano one foggy night while walking the streets of Saint John. Foulis also developed a coding system for the steam sound blasts that signalled distances to mariners and how to proceed to safety.

Foulis was a brilliant innovator but like other Maritimer inventors working in isolation, he was unable to capitalize on his genius. Without commercial instincts or access to financial support, he failed to patent his invention despite his recognition in New Brunswick as its creator. The steam fog horn was later patented by an American and used worldwide for almost a hundred years until radar and Loran were introduced to marine navigation. Foulis' invention was called the "Mariners Friend" by sailors but Foulis died in poverty in Saint John and was buried in an unmarked grave. In 1928, a bronze tablet recognizing Foulis' achievement was placed on the old Saint John Customs House by the federal government.

Sailing the Globe

The first person to **circumnavigate the globe** single-handedly was Captain Joshua Slocum, a boot-maker's son from Westport, Brier Island, Nova Scotia, between 1895 and 1898. An aging sailor of the wood and sail era, Slocum rebuilt an eleven-metre (37-foot) sloop, the *Spray*, in a derelict Massachusetts shipyard. He first tested the *Spray's* seaworthiness from Boston, homeward to Nova Scotia, before embarking on his epic solo voyage that undoubtedly stands as one of the greatest sea adventures of all time. Slocum's own account, *Sailing Alone Around the World*, was published in 1899 and is considered a masterpiece in narrative prose, one of the most fascinating literary stories ever written about life at sea.

Marine Gas Engines

No one is quite sure exactly when the two-cycle marine engines first appeared, but the early one-lunger gasoline engines were ideal for the isolated Maritime harbours and outports. Forman Hawboldt may have been the first to build a **marine gasoline engine** in the Maritimes when he successfully powered his way around Chester harbour amid cheers from the excited people of the small village.

Hawboldt established the Hawboldt Gas Engine Company about 1900, beginning by building the two-cylinder engines in his barn in Chester. Like most inventors, Forman Hawboldt displayed an early talent for finely de- tailed work and began his working career as a jeweller. But his mechanical interest in engines overtook his jewellery business when he began to design and build all the necessary parts for his engines, even establishing a foundry in his barn.

The simple, but highly reliable, engines designed for the inshore fishing boats proved popular and within fifteen years Hawboldt's company em- ployed about twenty-five men. By the Second World War, a faster, more powerful engine was required for longer fishing trips and the two-cycle engine declined in use, although the Hawboldt company continued to produce their famous Hawboldt engine.

Other important early marine engine manufacturers in the Maritimes were the Phoenix Foundry of Saint John with its Essex Gas Engine, as well as the Acadia Gas Engines of Bridgewater, considered at one time the largest marine engine manufacturers in Canada. The Lunenburg Foundry and Engineering was also very active in producing marine engines and remains so today. The Lunenburg company developed its most famous marine engine, the Atlantic, and according to one report, an Atlantic engine worked flawlessly for twenty-six years, covering over 160,000 kilometres (100,000 miles) for a Newfoundland fisherman who also used the engine to saw his wood each winter. After building over twelve thousand engines, the Lunen- burg Foundry is still in operation.

Steel Schooner James William

The first and only **all steel sailing schooner** built in Canada was the *James William*, a three-masted, 399 metric ton (440 ton) schooner, launched in 1908 by the J. W. Carmichael Company in New Glasgow on the East River. James Carmichael was a famous Pictou County industrialist who in 1809 became the first **merchant** in New Glasgow and later built many wooden vessels at his New Glasgow shipyard. Carmichael's brother-in-law and business associate, Captain George Rogers Mackenzie, was a renowned Bluenose shipbuilder and skipper, a man of great ability and seamanship. Mackenzie earned his sailing reputation by taking his windjammer, the *Hamilton-Cambell-Kidston*, up the shallow River Clyde to the city of Glasgow.

Carmichael died in 1860 and his son James W. continued to build wooden vessels but in 1883 began placing orders for iron ships with prominent Scottish shipyards on the Clyde River. The first **steel ship** built in Nova Scotia, the steamer *Mulgrave*, was launched in 1893 at the Carmichael shipyard as the Carmichael firm established a shipping fleet of steel ships including the first schooner.

Old Samson and the Flanger

The first **steam locomotive** in North America to burn coal and run over all-metal rails was the fifteen metric ton (17 ton) *Samson*, transporting coal at the Stellarton Albion Mines site in Pictou County. Built in England, the *Samson* travelled ten kilometres (6 miles) per hour and in 1839 began hauling coal to waiting ships at Abercrombie, along a ten-kilometre (6 mile) railway line of locally produced iron rails. The Scottish engineer, Donald Thompson, sat at the rear of the open locomotive, exposed to all kinds of weather. The Albion Mines railway was the second in Canada and the earliest to use a **standard gauge track and split-switch, movable rail**. In 1840, the Albion Mines railway became fully operational as a steam railway with three British built locomotives in service, *Samson*, *John Buddle* and the *Hercules*.

Prior to 1839, coal had been hauled along a tramway by horse-drawn rail cars. The cast-iron rails of this early line were also made at the Albion Mines. The historic rails are considered the first **iron rail line** to be manufactured in North America. The *Samson* was used for about thirty years, then exhibited at the 1893 World's Fair in Chicago and returned to Pictou County in 1950. Containing almost all its original parts, the *Samson* is North America's oldest surviving steam locomotive and the second oldest existing British Hackworth engine. The pioneer train is now on display at the Museum of Industry in Pictou County.

Another railway first was invented about 1874 by a Black Frederictonian railway worker, John Hamilton. Hamilton was described as a strong, versatile employee, able to perform most railway tasks, including building and maintaining equipment. The first known **railway flanger** for snow removal consisted of a pair of iron blades attached to the locomotive pilot that rode close to the rails and could be raised or lowered by a lever in the cab. The device was adopted as standard equipment on the old Number 2 locomotive of the Fredericton Railway Company which built and operated a branch line between Fredericton and Fredericton Junction, before becoming absorbed into the New Brunswick Railway.

The flanger began causing problems once stop signs were installed. The device was abandoned but not before it was patented. Records however, show that the Hamilton Flanger was actually patented as the Miller Flanger, named for the railway's branch engineer Henry Miller. It's not known whether New Brunswick was unwilling to issue patents to Blacks during the 1870s or if Hamilton sold his invention to Miller.

Wood and Steel Bridges

The **longest wooden covered bridge** in the world was completed in 1901 at Hartland, New Brunswick, over the Saint John River. Built over a two-year period, the wooden bridge spans 391 metres (1,282 feet) and was one of hundreds built throughout the Maritimes, especially in New Brunswick. A medical emergency caused Dr. Estey to be the first person to cross the bridge, one day prior to the official opening on May 14, 1901. To offset building expenses, tolls were charged during the first five years, three cents per person or per head of cattle, each way, while sheep were charged a half cent per head, each way.

The first **all-steel bridge** in Canada was erected in 1884 across the Reversing Falls on the Saint John River at Saint John. The cantilever railway bridge was constructed from imported steel and spanned the river for about

220 metres (722 feet). A roadway suspension bridge of wire cables and wood was also constructed nearby in 1853, by engineer William Reynolds, and remained in use until 1913. Tolls were initially collected at four cents per person, while a horse and carriage cost thirteen cents and rates for elephants or camels were posted at fifty cents each. A bargain however, could still be had by harbour ferry since the elephant could cross by water for twenty-five cents.

The Starr Manufacturing Company built the first iron bridge **fabricated in Canada** in 1877 and installed it the next year on the historic Intercolonial Railway line at Elmsdale, Nova Scotia. While the iron stock was imported from England, the bridge was built at Dartmouth for the federal government. The company also built the first **steel swing bridge** made in Canada, a sixty metre (190 foot) steel span inserted in the old wooden railway bridge across the narrows of Halifax harbour. Installed in 1884, the structure was destroyed in a 1892 storm and replaced but again collapsed the next year.

Variable Pitch Propeller

Wallace Turnbull invented the **variable pitch propeller**, often cited as the single most important invention in the history of aeronautics. A native of Rothesay, New Brunswick, Turnbull developed a working model of the propeller in 1916 and in 1927, with the Royal Canadian Air Force, tested it successfully in flight. By allowing the aircraft propeller blades to be adjusted in cutting through the wind, much like changing gears in a car, Turnbull's invention allowed for maximum efficiency and stability in flight, as well as during landing and take-off.

Called the father of aeronautical research in Canada, Turnbull was one of the rare Canadians able to work almost solely as an inventor. His variable pitch propeller is now at the National Aviation Museum in Ottawa and the Saint John Airport is named Turnbull Field. Turnbull sold the rights to his propeller in 1929 in order to pursue other interests.

He also built the first **wind tunnel** in Canada near Saint John in 1902 in order to conduct aviation tests and built a private railway track, installing a trolley to test fixed-pitch propellers. One of Canada's leading aviation pioneers, Turnbull died in New Brunswick in 1954, while working with an idea he had spent almost forty years on, harnessing the tides of the Bay of Fundy for electrical generation.

Flight

While Canada's first **balloon ascension** reportedly took place at Saint John in 1840, the first **airplane flight** in Canada, about one kilometre (.6 miles) at twenty metres (57 feet) in height, was undertaken by J.A.D. (Douglas) McCurdy. It occurred in February 1909, over the Bras d'Or Lakes at Baddeck, aboard his aircraft, the *Silver Dart*. McCurdy, along with Casey Baldwin, members of Alexander Graham Bell's Aerial Experiment Association, were attempting to build gas-powered engines for flight. The *Silver Dart* was their fourth airplane.

McCurdy spent his life testing the limits of the new air age and was the first to undertake an **ocean flight**, from Florida to Cuba, where he became the first pilot to be **rescued at sea** when his plane crashed in the ocean, sixteen kilometres (10 miles) from Havana, the result of a faulty oil connection. McCurdy was the first to **send and receive messages** in flight and also the first Canadian to obtain a **pilot's licence**. After a career in the aircraft industry, McCurdy returned to Nova Scotia in 1947 to become its lieutenant-governor. Today a full-size replica of the *Silver Dart*, built in 1984 by Baddeck craftsmen to celebrate the seventy-fifth anniversary of the historic flight, is on display at the Atlantic Canada Aviation Museum, near Halifax International Airport.

McCurdy's colleague at Baddeck, Casey Baldwin, had become the first **Canadian** and seventh person to fly a controlled flight a year earlier in 1908, when he flew ninety-seven metres (318 feet) over the ice at Hammondsport, New York, aboard the *Red Wing*. The next year, Dolly MacLeod became the first **female to fly** in an airplane when she flew approximately five kilometres (3 miles) with Casey Baldwin, aboard the *Silver Dart* at Baddeck Bridge.

Aviation Research Team

The concept of a research team of specialists focusing on various aspects of a single problem or task was first pioneered in 1907 by Alexander Graham Bell at Baddeck, Cape Breton. Inventions during the Victorian era were typically undertaken by brilliant innovators working in isolation, often approaching a technical puzzle without additional expertise. Independently wealthy from his telephone work, as well as his wife's inheritance, Bell began to experiment with kites and balloons, becoming fascinated with the possibilities of flight. He began to assemble a team of engineers with special skills, capable of tackling various aspects of the complex problems surrounding human flight.

Bell's **Aerial Experiment Association** (AEA) was composed of the young engineers Douglas McCurdy and Casey Baldwin, as well as a motorcycle engine manufacturer Glenn H. Curtiss, and US Army aeronautics expert Lieutenant Thomas Selfridge. Tom Selfridge was later killed in an airplane crash in Virginia while flying with Orville Wright. Bell described his aerial dream team as "brilliant young men each an expert in his own line." Their mission was put bluntly by Selfridge: "All we want to do is get into the air." Initially financed by Mabel Bell, the AEA group conducted many aerial experiments including building a number of primitive aircraft and in 1909, McCurdy succeeded in becoming the first person to fly a gasoline-powered aircraft in the British Empire.

Having accomplished its goal of powered flight, the AEA was dissolved the same year. Bell later established the first **aircraft manufacturing company** in Canada, the Canadian Aerodrome Company, set up to build aerodromes commercially. The commercial operation was ahead of its time and proved unsuccessful, since its chief client, the Canadian military, deemed the aircraft too dangerous. All their experiments did not produce successful results but Bell's research team did succeed in pioneering the first powered flights in Canada. Bell's concept of a group of specialists working together on common experiments or problems is today standard scientific practice.

Hydrofoil Achievements

The idea of boats with slanted ladders of blades for floating above the water had been worked on in Europe since 1861. But Alexander Graham Bell seems to have been the first to realize the potential of **hydrofoil** for marine transportation. At Baddeck with Casey Baldwin, he began experimenting in 1903 and by 1908 had developed one of the most successful hydrofoil boats, the *Dhonnas Beag* (the *Little Devil*).

Based on the notion that air offers less resistance than water, they pioneered a watercraft with a submerged set of wings that supported the boat and once increased speed was reached, lifted the boat's hull out of the water. Driven by air propellers, the *Dhonnas Beag* lifted about a foot clear of the water on October 20, 1908, considered the first **pure hydrofoil achievement**.

In 1919 at Baddeck Bay, their *HD-4* reached a world record speed of 113 kilometres (70.86 miles) per hour a record not broken until 1929. Bell originally saw the hydrofoil as a potential flying machine but later became convinced of its potential as a high-speed naval vessel capable of intercepting submarines. The original *Flying 400* boat is on display at the Alexander Graham Bell Museum in Baddeck.

In 1968 in Halifax harbour, an experimental warship began to be tested. *HMCS Bras d'Or* became Canada's first **naval hydrofoil**, although the Canadian Navy had been experimenting with the hydrofoil concept since 1918. A naval ship, *HMCS Patriot* had towed one of Bell's early hydrofoil vessels around the Bras d'Or lakes during the 1920s. Due to excessive design costs as well as the judgement that the *Bras d'Or* offered limited military capabilities, the navy abandoned the hydrofoil project.

Business

"I guess I know as much about building canoes as anyone. I was at it for fifty-five years and my father built Chestnuts twenty-three years before me. As long as the Company takes the time and uses good wood, nobody will build a better canoe." — Merle Burse, Chestnut Canoe builder.

Oldest Board of Trade

The first **trade organization** in Canada, and perhaps in North America, was established at Halifax in 1750, one year after the garrison town's founding. Unable to adequately support newly arrived settlers, the governor and his council sought the assistance of merchants, who, according to T.B. Akins in his *History of Halifax*, "at this early period had formed themselves into an association for the benefit of trade." The Halifax Board Of Trade was founded by Halifax merchants to petition Britain on matters of currency, shipping, and other commercial matters, and today, remains the oldest such association in existence in Canada.

Known by various names, including the Halifax Committee of Trade, the Guild of Merchants, the Nova Scotia Commercial Society, as well as the more recent Halifax Board of Trade, the early board often applied unrelenting pressure in determining local commercial policy and in swaying British trade policy toward the Maritimes. Their domination of the early local councils, together with their British connections, meant their views on trade matters often became official policy.

While their attempt to exclude American ships from the early carrying trade to the West Indies was successful if shortlived, the Board of Trade did manage to achieve many of its goals in other important areas, such as the fishery, coal trade, agriculture and custom tariffs, often at the expense of other Maritime communities. Holding regular meetings at Halifax's early meeting chambers, the Pontac Inn, or the Merchants' Exchange, this commercial association was largely responsible for the early economic development of Halifax.

Royal City Market

In a 1785 Royal Charter incorporating Saint John as a city, a common-law **commercial market** was also granted, making it the oldest covered market still in operation in British North America. The historic market, occupying a full city block from Charlotte Street to Germain Street, survived the Great Fire of 1877 despite the destruction of many adjoining buildings.

A popular and somewhat unique institution, the Victorian market building was constructed with hand-hewn timbers inspired by ship carpenters and features massive roof supports, resembling the inverted hull of a ship, a tribute to Saint John's shipbuilding past. Large iron gates are situated at either end of the city block that encompasses the market where local delicacies such as salmon, fiddleheads and dulse are featured. The Slocum and Ferris shop was first established in 1894 by merchant George Slocum.

Fire and Marine Insurance

Protection of property against loss by fire or shipwreck at sea seems to have been the main concern of citizens in early British North America. Merchants and shipowners involved in trade formed the Halifax Marine Society in 1786, the first **Canadian marine insurance company**. Members met quarterly at Mrs. Sutherland's Coffee House in Halifax and in 1794 agreed to jointly underwrite policies of insurance on vessels and cargo, appointing Benjamin Salter as their broker. Marine insurance had previously been considered a monopoly for British companies but a similar company was established in 1801 at Saint John. The oldest known **chartered marine insurance company** in the Maritimes was the Nova Scotia Marine Insurance Company, which formed in 1835 and offered protection of property loss at sea.

The earliest Canadian **fire insurance company** was also started in Halifax, in 1809, and received its corporate charter in 1819. As the first domestic insurer against the dreaded fire hazard, the Halifax Fire Insurance Company attempted to obtain a monopoly with its charter by agreeing to fix premiums but nevertheless had to compete for business against agents for British companies. Located in the Hollis Street house of its secretary, J. H. Fleigher, the fire company insured buildings, furniture and other personal goods but lost heavily during a rash of local fires in the 1850s. The company managed to survive by recruiting additional investors and continued to operate well into the twentieth century.

Halifax Currency

The first currency to be established in British North America was the semi-official "**Halifax currency.**" During the early colonial period, many competing currencies were in circulation including French money, British sterling, Spanish dollars, as well as a number of local currencies, including the first North American paper currency printed in Massachusetts in 1690 called Boston bills.

The early local paper currencies were often not redeemable, or heavily discounted, outside the area in which they were issued. With British reluctance to export sterling to North America, money was scarce. Common currency and fair trading value was a difficult issue throughout North America, including the Maritimes. Use of the barter system was widespread with commodities such as wheat, corn and tobacco used as trading tender. The first currency was probably beaver pelts where .453 kilograms (1 pound) of top beaver fur was reported to be worth five shillings.

Coinage was particularly sought after and the Spanish silver dollar was in wide circulation throughout the West Indies, American colonies and the Canadian provinces. Yet confusion often prevailed in trading matters since all the colonies kept their official accounts in British pounds. About 1756 the term Halifax Currency became common in fixing the Spanish dollar as being worth five shillings. No other coins or means of using decimals of a dollar other than shillings and pence existed. Boston currency paid six shillings per dollar and with twenty shillings per British pound, Halifax Currency valued a pound at four dollars.

The use of Halifax Currency to establish a common monetary unit was widespread and lasted well into the 1800s, after the Spanish dollar had ceased to be traded. Merchants at Quebec in 1764 had petitioned the governor to continue to use the Halifax Currency as the standard currency, fearing further confusion if a new standard was adopted. Their fears may have been confirmed. In 1777 Quebec enacted a new currency law based on the Halifax standard. By about 1825, copper pennies and half-pennies began to be minted in large amounts or imported, but in addition to shortages counterfeiting became a problem.

Holey Dollar

An ingenious solution to the chronic shortages of coinage appeared in Prince Edward Island in 1813 when Lieutenant Governor Charles Smith arrived to find the "want of a circulating medium one of the most prominent evils that struck me on my arrival." To prevent the export of its metal currency, Smith issued "**holey money**" by punching a hole in Spanish silver dollars and declaring the outer ring acceptable at face value.

But the cut centres were also valued at one shilling each and, although His Excellency limited the cut currency to one thousand, counterfeit coins appeared almost immediately. Since the sum total of the cut dollars were worth more than the uncut versions, fraud became rampant and almost immediately the Executive Council withdrew the cut dollars from circulation. Today, the counterfeit cut dollars are extremely rare. At a public auction in 1973, a Prince Edward Island holey dollar sold for $2,300.

Banking

Canada's first government authorized **chartered bank**, The Bank of New Brunswick, was established in Saint John in 1820 by the city's merchant and Loyalist elite. The bank's official charter was granted by the provincial government and institutionalized banking began in British North America. The first president was Saint John Mayor and Loyalist John Robinson. Board members included future Supreme Court chief justices Ward Chipman, Jr. and Robert Parker, Jr.

The original Bank of New Brunswick building at 71 Prince William Street was destroyed in the Great Fire of 1877 and rebuilt on the same site. The old New Brunswick Bank was amalgamated with the Bank Of Nova Scotia in 1913 and business continued at the Prince William site until 1977 when the Bank Of Nova Scotia moved to its present location in Brunswick Square on King Street.

The Bank Of Montreal actually began operations in 1817, before the Bank of New Brunswick but was not chartered until 1822. A private savings bank, the Collins Bank, was established in 1825 by merchants Enos Collins and Samuel Cunard, and the old stone structure now forms part of Halifax's Historic Properties. The bank had no charter and its capital holdings and public liability unknown since its operations were kept secret. Robbed a number of times, the amount stolen was never revealed. The Collins Bank was not well used by Nova Scotians and closed as chartered banks were formed.

Canada's second oldest existing bank, The Bank Of Nova Scotia, was founded in Halifax in 1832, and used the New Brunswick Bank as its model. Scotiabank still maintains its head office in Halifax while its main office has since moved to Toronto. The **largest bank** in Canada, the Royal Bank, was also started in Halifax, in 1864, as the Merchants Bank Of Halifax.

Marine Salvage Expedition

The first **commercial underwater salvage** using a diver's helmet in North America occurred off Prince Edward Island in July 1842. John Fraser of Pictou (whose partner and brother J.D.B. Fraser produced the first chloroform in Canada), had been working in undersea salvage for Lloyd's off the coast of Germany and returned to Pictou, equipped with a modern diving helmet.

Fraser and another Pictou diver, Alexander Munro, salvaged thirty-five cannons from the *HMS Mallabar* off Cape Bear, Prince Edward Island. Diving helmets had been invented by Siebe in 1819 and Fraser was described as wearing a large, heavy headgear with three windows and an air intake tube coming in from above, with the discharge outlet below the helmet. Fraser was also weighed down with about fifty-four kilograms (120 pounds) of lead in his waterproof rubber suit and reportedly spent thirty minutes in five metres (18 feet) of water and later went as deep as eleven metres (36 feet) in Pictou harbour. The compensation paid by the British government for the salvage venture was less than satisfactory to the Fraser brothers and they ceased further salvage expeditions.

Lumber, Pulp and Paper

North America's first **sawmill**, a waterpowered pit mill, was erected in 1612 by Port Royal colonists at Lequille, on the Allains River, near Annapolis Royal. A grist mill had been built earlier and the mill employed a web, steel-blade saw fastened in a wooden frame in order to saw logs lengthwise into lumber. Power was conveyed to the saw by means of a rod connected to a waterwheel and with water readily available throughout the Maritimes, waterpowered mills slowly began to appear in every nook and cranny along the east coast. By 1861, the number of working sawmills had peaked with Nova Scotia reporting 1,401 in its enumerated census and New Brunswick 689.

Commercial lumbering operation also began in Nova Scotia near present day Riverport. There in 1632, Nicolas Denys built a residence and began shipping LaHave River oak to France. Denys continued to produce sawn planks for export until his friend and ally Isaac de Razilly died and was replaced as lieutenant-governor by a new governor who was hostile to Denys' lumbering efforts. Denys moved to the Bay of Chaleur, establishing a trading post and then to Cape Breton, where he became governor of the island. With his work, *The Description and Natural History of the Coasts of North America*, Denys produced one of the most detailed accounts of the Maritimes during the seventeenth century.

Another pioneering effort involving Maritime lumber is the development of wood paper. Charles Fenerty succeeded in producing **paper from pulp fibre** at Upper Sackville, Nova Scotia, in 1841 and perhaps as early as 1838. Paper had previously been produced from cotton or linen and by the mid 1800s was in short supply throughout the world. Rags had become so scarce that as late as 1818, it was a criminal offence in England to make newspapers larger than fifty-six by eighty-one centimetres (22 by 32 inches). A rag paper mill had been established by the printer-publisher Anthony Holland near Bedford Basin in 1819. Yet even in Nova Scotia, Holland had difficulty acquiring the cotton and linen he needed for papermaking.

The inventor of wood newsprint reportedly got the idea when he noticed wasps chewing wood fibre and producing a kind of paper for their nests. It was reported that Fenerty took home an abandoned wasp's nest and examined it under a magnifying glass. Another theory is that Fenerty got the idea for pulp paper by observing during his work in local sawmills, the tiny spruce fibres produced by the friction of wood on wood. Fenerty would have noticed that the spruce fibre was similar to the composition of the vegetable fibre of cotton.

Fenerty began experimenting by grinding spruce fibre and gradually got better results until a usable newsprint evolved. Although Fenerty's newsprint was produced by primitive methods and cannot be considered commercial quality, he did pioneer the paper from ground pulp process in North America. Around the same time, other inventors on the American continent were reported to have made paper from chemically treated wood.

Fenerty's discovery was not well publicized until 1844 when the *Acadian Recorder* published his letter outlining the procedure he had invented. Considered an eccentric dreamer, Fenerty failed to continue to refine his papermaking process and a patent was not acquired, although the German weaver Friedrich Kellor had applied to register a similar process in 1840 and is generally credited with inventing pulp paper. Kellor did secure a German patent for a wood-grinding machine that became the basis for most wood ground paper products for the next fifty years.

More interested in literary pursues than business, Fenerty did not gain any financial rewards from his contributions to such an important industrial innovation nor did he receive any recognition for his achievement during his lifetime. His invention however, became the cornerstone of the modern pulp and paper industry which today is Canada's largest manufacturing industry and paper its biggest export.

Another lumbering landmark was Canada's first **sulphite pulp mill**, built in 1885 for the Halifax Wood Fibre Company at Sheet Harbour by lumber baron William Chisholm. Building on the East River, near one of his sawmills, Chisholm hauled his spruce slabs on horse-drawn cars to his new mill where the slabs were debarked, chipped and cooked with sulphurous liquid in the digesters. Each ton of air-dried pulp required about 1,406 kilograms (3,100 pounds) of chipped wood, that was then pressed into bales and shipped by schooner to New England.

An average day produced about eight tons of finished pulp and Chisholm's new lumbering operation was successful until an 1890 US import tariff of six dollars per ton made the pulp unprofitable to produce. Unable to find other markets, Canada's first sulphite pulp mill closed in 1891.

Starr Manufacturing, the Skate Company

John Starr founded the Starr Manufacturing Company in Dartmouth in 1861, producing nuts, bolts, and screws. His foreman, John Forbes, an inventive machinist, and a co-worker, Thomas Bateman, soon designed a metal spring skate that eliminated the use of straps. By producing the world's first **steel ice skates**, the Starr Company became one of the most successful manufacturers in Canada.

Patented in 1866 by John Forbes and produced at his Prince Albert Road manufacturing plant, the Acme spring skate sold for seventy five cents a pair and had a revolutionary effect on skating and the newly emerging sport of hockey. While existing wooden skates were known to split if made to stop suddenly, the spring skates could be attached to or released from any boot by means of a clamp and lever, without heavy straps or buckles cramping the foot or ankle. With its short, lightweight blade and ease of use, the spring skate was ideal for fancy skating on small ice surfaces and led to the popular indoor rinks and skating carnivals of the Victorian era.

Located near the Dartmouth canal stream within sight of the harbour, the factory was ideally situated to receive raw supplies and ship finished skates. Over three million pairs of skates were shipped worldwide during the 1860s and in its peak year, 1873, the company employed 250 people and reported profits of $25,000. The company celebrated by presenting the wife of the Governor General, Lady Dufferin, with a pair of gold plated skates. The Starr Company also produced its famous Micmac brand of hockey sticks but later lost the skate patent by failing to renew it on time. The skate market was opened up to rival firms, although the company continued to manufacture skates until 1938. In all, eleven million pairs of skates were known to have been produced.

Thomas Hall's Farm Machinery

One of the earliest manufacturers of **Maritime farm machinery** was Thomas Hall of Wilmot, PEI. As early as 1859, Hall was building threshing machines for export from his three-storey factory in Summerside. Many popular implements were produced, including the Eureka that served as a combination fanning mill and seed separator, as well as mowers, reapers and seed sowers. But Hall's fame was firmly secured by his carefully crafted threshing machine that won first prize at the 1881 Dominion Exhibition in Halifax.

But the thresher's popularity was a two-edged sword since Hall was constantly unable to meet the demand for his first-class machine. Production rarely exceeded sixty units per year. The National Policy and tariff law favouring Canadian production was instituted in 1879 and initially assisted Hall's efforts to be competitive. But the entrepreneur was soon challenged by large central Canadian manufacturers even for his home market. Ontario firms such as the Masseys, with access to capital and improved machinery technology, were able to render his locally crafted machines obsolete. Yet Thomas Hall himself was an innovator of genius, especially in adapting existing manufacturing designs for farm machinery to meet local needs and conditions. He retired around 1914 as his business became more of an agency for outside equipment sales than a farm production facility.

Cotton Mill

Whether its proximity to the Yankee traders, Loyalist background or simply an entrepreneurial spirit developed out of the Fundy tides, Saint John became the undisputed commercial centre of the Maritimes during the nineteenth century. Once they sensed opportunity, the businessmen of Saint John were not afraid of taking a risk with their capital.

One such risk-taker was William Parks. He arrived in Saint John in 1822 from Northern Ireland and by the late 1840s had become wealthy from his merchant and shipping interests, especially in trade with the West Indies. Parks also was involved with James Fleming at the Phoenix Foundry in constructing the first **locomotives** in the Maritimes.

In 1861 Parks erected the first **cotton mill** in the Maritimes, a three-storey brick structure on Wall Street, complete with twenty-four looms producing grey cotton fabric. He began by bringing in weavers from Britain and New England, but purchased yarn from England where it had been spun from southern American cotton. When the American Civil War broke out, Union forces erected a naval blockade of the South, preventing cotton exports from reaching Britain. Sensing his mill threatened by a severe shortage of materials, Parks acted quickly. He installed carding and spinning machinery in order to spin the cotton into yarn and then hired Saint John windships to run the blockade in and out of Southern ports, bringing American cotton back to Saint John.

William Parks & Son also established another mill called the New Brunswick Cotton Mill and by the 1890s had become one of the largest employers in Saint John with almost thirty thousand spindles operated by about five hundred people. Parks' son, John, expanded the business under Macdonald's National Policy and also constructed another mill at Courtenay Bay where the structure remained until 1994. The company was reorganized as the Cornwall & York Cotton Mills in 1903 and eventually was purchased by Canadian Cottons Ltd. Parks himself met an unexpected fate in 1870 when he sailed to England on the mysterious steamer, the *City of Boston*. The ship, its crew and all passengers were never heard from again, presumably lost at sea in the vicinity of Sable Island.

Brown Box Company

D. F. Brown was a Boston merchant who had noted the increased business opportunities after a serious fire had destroyed a portion of Boston. After hearing of Saint John's Great Fire of 1877, Brown arrived in New Brunswick determined to establish a business. He began by erecting a plant at Union and Waterloo streets hoping to manufacture paper bags since he knew of a new machine recently introduced in Massachusetts, capable of eliminating the obsolete hand manufacturing process still in use in Canada. But Brown was beaten to the Canadian rights by an Upper Canadian firm and instead, in 1878, bought machinery from Boston for producing the first **paper boxes** in Canada.

No other company in Canada was producing these boxes at the time and demand grew, especially among the many small Maritime shoe companies in operation at the time. Brown's son opened a branch plant in Halifax and demand continued for their stiff, durable boxes for packing and shipping until the folding cardboard boxes began to appear after the First World War.

Chestnut Canoe Company

Beginning in 1875, E.H. Gerrish of Bangor, Maine, became the first commercial company to build wood and canvas canoes. By the turn of the century, the Old Town Canoe Company of Maine was also active in pioneering the construction of canoes, made of woven hard canvas stretched over cedar frames.

In Canada, the Chestnut brothers, William and Harry, were successful businessmen in Fredericton, operating their family hardware company that had been in business since 1832 at Phoenix Square under the sign: "We fear nae foe." In 1899, not content with importing Maine canoes, they hired a local carpenter, Jack Moore, and began building these new canoes for the Canadian market. Most early canvas canoes were fashioned with cedar ribs that were steamed and bent over wooden forms with planking fastened to the ribs and covered with canvas.

In 1904, Harry struck gold by managing to patent the **wood and canvas canoe** construction technique for the entire Dominion of Canada. As the only Canadian company able to construct canvas canoes, the Chestnut brothers began experiencing a sharp demand for these light but durable boats, first produced with wood and bark by the North American Indians. In order to increase production, William Chestnut was able to convince a number of experienced Old Town Canoe employees to move to Fredericton and work for Chestnut.

Competing directly against the Ontario based Peterborough Canoe Company, who had pioneered the all-wood canoe during the 1860s, the Chestnut canoe became the most popular canoe in Canada. In time, over a hundred different models and styles of canoes were produced from more than sixty forms. In 1907, the Chestnut Canoe Company was incorporated as the brothers moved from their cramped quarters near their hardware store to a new factory on York Street. In order to maintain its patent, the Chestnut company fought a lawsuit that challenged its Canadian monopoly and was able to secure its product throughout Canada. The Chestnut replaced the Peterborough wood canoe as the favourite canoe of the Hudson Bay Company's vast northern retail operations. By 1915, the Hudson Bay Company was buying all the canoes Chestnut could make. Nicknamed the

The Chestnut Canoe Company's early factory location on King Street, Fredericton, about 1904. (George Taylor, New Brunswick Public Archives)

"workhouse of the north," the Chestnut became world famous as the company became the largest canoe manufacturer in Canada, producing small four metre and five metre (14 and 16 feet) canoes as well as larger canoes, including the eight metre (25 feet) freighters.

Two fires in the 1920s caused serious setbacks to the Chestnut operation but each time, the company came back, producing a wide range of canoes, as well as paddles, toboggans, and snowshoes. Harry Chestnut ran the business until his death in 1941 when his daughter, Maggie Jean, and wife Annie T., became the last Chestnuts to operate the company.

The Chestnut Canoe Company continued to experience strong demand for its canoes until the introduction of fibreglass canoes in the 1960s. They continued to operate their historic York Street facility until 1975. Unable to fully compete with synthetic canoes, the company was forced to close. The Chestnut canoe forms are now dispersed among various canoe builders throughout North America where the Chestnut models are still being produced.

Silver Fox Ranching

The first fox ranchers to successfully breed the rare **silver fox** were entrepreneurs Charles Dalton and Robert Oulton in 1896 at Alberton, Prince Edward Island. Establishing fox kennels that resembled the animal's natural breeding habitat, Dalton and Oulton patiently and secretly learned the animal's diet and habits until they successfully bred captive silver black foxes. Dispensing with the old hollow log dens, Oulton learned to domesticate wild foxes in his fox pens. Dalton provided the business acumen, and together the two established the fox industry in Canada.

The industry remained tightly controlled by a small group of Island entrepreneurs led by Dalton until 1910, when a member sold a pair of foxes to outsiders, opening up the fox farming industry. By the turn of the century, silver fox pelts were very valuable furs and the eastern Prince Edward Island industry was worth about $20 million annually. Dalton made a fortune with his fox-breeding expertise and in 1931 became the lieutenant governor of Prince Edward Island.

During the peak years in the 1920s, a pair of silver foxes reportedly sold for $35,000 and the industry constituted a staggering seventeen per cent of the Island's economy. In 1920, Summerside became the headquarters of the Canadian National Silver Fox Breeder's Association, but by the 1940s overproduction as well as outside competition caused this highly profitable Island industry to collapse. The International Fox Museum & Hall of Fame in Summerside depicts the fox fur industry worldwide, as well as the men and women of Prince Edward Island responsible for establishing and developing this unique industry.

Fuller Brush Man

The first company to successfully sell consumer products door-to-door on a mass scale was the **Fuller Brush Company**, established by Alfred C. Fuller of Kings County, Nova Scotia. Born in 1885 at Welsford, Fuller moved to New England in 1906 and made brushes at night then sold them door-to-door during the day.

By 1923, Fuller Brush became a household name in North America with hundreds of sales representatives knocking on doors from California to Newfoundland and annual sales exceeding $15 million. At the company's peak in the 1950s, more than 2,700 people were employed with sales in excess of $110 million. Fuller's autobiography, *A Foot in the Door*, was published in 1960. He died in New England in 1973.

Steel Making

Pictou County became the **birthplace of steel** in Canada when in 1883, two New Glasgow blacksmiths, Graham Fraser and Forrest MacKay, formed the Nova Scotia Steel Company, producing the country's first steel. Previous attempts at making steel in Canada had occurred in various locations, including St. Maurice, Quebec and Londonderry, Nova Scotia. With railway production at its peak, the market for steel was expanding rapidly and Fraser travelled to Europe and the US to learn the steelmaking process. The Trenton company began by employing about 160 men, manufacturing the Siemens Martin brand of steel which involved a process of melting pig iron along with iron and steel scraps.

Initially the pig iron necessary for steel was imported from Scotland but within ten years, the ambitious Fraser had formed the New Glasgow Iron, Coal and Railway Company in order to produce the pig iron from local iron ore, limestone, and Pictou County coal. A blast furnace was constructed at Ferrona as were coke ovens.

After visiting German steel makers, Fraser also built North America's first **coal washing plant** in order to reduce the sulphur content of the coal before coking. Fraser's insistence on washing the high sulphur Pictou coal despite much opposition showed brilliant foresight, since without it the Nova Scotia steel industry could not have used local coal. By 1912, under the management of Thomas Cantley, the Nova Scotia Steel and Coal Company was one of Canada's largest enterprises, producing fifty per cent of the steel annually consumed in Canada and employing at its peak 6,500 men. With a modern steel complex in place, as well as an iron and coal industry, shipbuilding, glassworks, tanneries, manufacturing factories, and a thriving lumber trade, Pictou County became one of Canada's earliest centres of heavy industry during the late-1800s.

Thomas Cantley became president of the Nova Scotia Steel and Coal Corporation in 1915 and provided an important contribution to the munitions war effort during World War I by being the first steel company in

Canada to produce steel suitable for **encasing military shells**. Ironically the fourteen million shells forged in Trenton for use against the Germans were produced on a German made, hydraulic steel press.

More than any other individual, Graham Fraser was responsible for industrial development in Pictou County. He had also started the Nova Scotia Forge Company with Forrest MacKay at Trenton, manufacturing rail and marine iron works, including railway cars, axles and anchors. As the Eastern Car Works, most railway freight cars in Canada were produced at Trenton and today Trenton Works is still producing rail cars.

As Pictou County iron ore became depleted, Fraser acquired control of the huge iron ore deposits at Wabana in Newfoundland and, together with Cape Breton coal and limestone, began making steel ingots at Sydney Mines, while continuing to roll and forge steel at Trenton. Disappointed with the steel operation at Sydney Mines, Graham Fraser resigned as managing director of Nova Scotia Steel in 1903 and briefly became manager of the huge Dominion Iron and Steel complex at Sydney. With its huge inventory of coal deposits, Cape Breton became one of Canada's most important industrial centres, manufacturing large quantities of steel throughout the twentieth century. Fraser returned to New Glasgow where he briefly served as the town's mayor, passing away on Christmas Day, 1915, at age sixty-nine.

Shatter-Proof Rails

The world's first **shatter-free railway rails** were produced at Sydney, in July of 1931, when 4,082 metric tons (4,500 tons) were rolled for the Canadian Pacific Railway. Internal cracks in new rails had been a mystery in modern steel fabrication and the cause of many accidents since the cracks were often hidden inside the rails with no indication on the surface of their weakness. I. Cameron Mackie, a metallurgist at Sydney's Dominion Steel & Coal Corporation, discovered that rail cracks were not the result of high temperature as had been previously thought.

The cracks were formed in the rails at lower temperature and Mackie's solution was to control and retard the cooling process further. He succeeded in eliminating the cracks without softening the rails and in 1932 patented his results as the "Retarded Rail Cooling Process." By the 1940s most rail producers worldwide were using the Mackie cooling method to manufacture rails, including a number of US companies that Mackie had successfully sued for patent infringement. In recognition of his accomplishment, Mackie was granted honourary membership in the Canadian Standards Association.

Car Assembly Plant

The first **European car** assembled in Canada was driven off the assembly line in Dartmouth, June 11, 1963 by Prince Bertil of Sweden. Volvo picked Dartmouth for its first overseas car plant because it viewed Halifax harbour as one of the nearest North American ice-free ports to Sweden. The B-18 series, 122 model Volvo was the first car produced outside Sweden and was presented to the Province of Nova Scotia. For three years the car received the first licence number issued in Nova Scotia and now forms part of the collection of the Museum of Industry in Pictou County.

Food and drink

"We did it, we showed them how, and in the opinion of the industry on the Atlantic coast, the continuation of what we started in Toronto was killed deliberately by the wholesale fish dealer who distribute the fish. He was against it, because it was competition with the stale fish he sold."
— A.G. Huntsman, commenting bitterly on the Atlantic fish industry's resistance to his pioneering quick-frozen fish fillets. *The Aquatic Explorers* by Kenneth Johnstone.

Native and European Agriculture

The original peoples of eastern Canada were semi-nomadic, living in extended family groups and gathering seasonal food supplies. With abundant food found throughout the rivers and forests of the Maritimes, there may have been little incentive to plant seeds or cultivate livestock. Plants, fish, birds and other wild animals provided for the needs of the aboriginials, but it is known that **corn, squash, beans** and perhaps **tobacco**, were grown.

The birthplace of **European agriculture** in North America is generally acknowledged to be Port Royal. Marc Lescarbot, who lived at Port Royal, wrote of growing rye, barley, oats, beans, and other garden vegetables, in his *History of New France*. The first **horticulturist** was Doctor Louis Hébert, who was primarily interested in growing medicinal herbs while in Acadia. The first wheat was successfully sown in 1606 and initially the bread grain was ground by hand, a task so difficult that some settlers reportedly preferred to go without bread than grind the wheat themselves. The next year a water-driven **grist mill**, the first in America, was erected by Seigneur de Poutrincourt, at Lequille, near the mouth of the Allains River. A Nova Scotia Power plant is now located at the site, disguised as Poutrincourt's original mill.

Acadian Dykelands — the Aboiteau

About 1630, France began to more fully colonize Acadia. Early European settlements located around the rich marshlands of the Bay of Fundy were unlike the rest of North America. Settlers did not timber the uplands and plant crops, but dyked and drained the saltmarshes to create a unique agricultural-based colony. Sediment from the highest tides in the world had left a fertile, rich soil and the Acadian settlers soon discovered that the new dykelands produced abundant crops annually without need for fertilizer.

The Acadians either invented the **aboiteau** or brought the technology from France. They used it to drain the marshes, first at Port Royal and gradually all Fundy Bay marshlands, amounting to thousands of acres. By 1970, 33,184 hectares (82,000 acres) had been reclaimed. The aboiteau, a log sluice attached with a hinged gate inside it, drained fresh water from above at low tide but would close at high tide to prevent saltwater from entering the marsh. The aboiteau was placed in the tidal creek bed and covered with sod to form part of the dyke that was constructed and maintained above the high water line.

The development of the Maritime dykelands closely corresponded to the early settlements of the Maritimes. After the expulsion of the Acadians, most fertile dykelands were occupied by New England Planters and Loyalists for agricultural production. During the nineteenth century, two large-scale dyke-building projects were completed at Canard, the Wellington Dyke, and at Aulac, the Etter Aboiteau, bringing into production hundreds of new acres of marshlands. These ancient dykelands, some of the earliest **commercial agricultural land** in Canada, are still maintained today.

Rum Distillery

In 1751 Joshua Mauger erected the first known **rum distillery** in Canada on the Halifax waterfront near the naval dockyard. Much of the operating revenue for the new settlement of Halifax was to have been derived from import duties on liquors, especially rum, but once established at five pence per gallon, little rum was legally imported into the colony. Mauger's operation and another distillery started by John Fillis in 1752 quickly began to produce most of the rum consumed in the province at the expense of the provincial treasury.

Smuggling rum also became a popular activity, but when Governor Campbell moved to reduce the tariff to three pence per gallon in hopes of promoting West Indies trade and increasing provincial revenues, Mauger managed to block the move using his powerful lobby of politically connected friends in London.

Despite moving to England, Mauger's monopoly on the rum trade remained intact as he began to dominate the province's economic life. His extensive property holdings, interests in shipping and the coastal carrying trade made Mauger the king-pin of the mercantile elite in Halifax, who were seen by local authorities as profiting at the expense of the economic development of the province.

Agricultural Fair

Windsor, Nova Scotia, on May 21, 1765, held the first known **agricultural exhibition** in North America, featuring a showing of cattle, sheep, horses, hogs, grain, as well as farm produce such as butter, cheese and homespun cloth. Planning for the fair and its original charter began a year earlier when Windsor Township was created. Wrestling, shooting and running events were also included and the following year, horse racing was added with the result that Windsor became prominent throughout Nova Scotia for its race track and fast horses.

While the fair languished around 1800, it was revived with a new fair charter in 1815 and the annual exhibition still continues. A monument unveiled in 1935 by the Historic Sites and Monuments Board of Canada commemorates the fair's historic site at Fort Edward, overlooking Windsor and the Minas Basin.

First Biscuit Factory

A young baker named Thomas Rankine left Scotland in 1824 on a windjammer and landed at Saint John. Within a few months he had opened a small shop on Church Street, producing sea biscuits for sale. Within two years, Rankine had erected a large building on Mill Street and established T. Rankine Sons Limited, considered Canada's first **biscuit factory**. Sea biscuits or "hard tack," as it was referred to by sailors, was the early freeze-dried food of mariners, essential to all ships without baking facilities.

Rankine produced all his biscuits by hand until 1844, importing flour from Britain. He enjoyed unloading the cargo himself and carrying it on his back to Mill Street. Often he could be seen visiting the captains of the square-riggers, taking orders for his hard biscuits. Sometimes as much as a full ton would be ordered for voyages around the world.

Rankine's baking business grew rapidly. By 1875 it was considered the **largest bakery** in Canada with three plants in operation, despite having a market mainly concentrated in the Maritimes, Newfoundland and the West Indies. The company diversified into other baked lines, including soda crackers, breads, molasses and sugar cookies but continued to produce its famous hard tack.

As Rankine's sons became actively involved in the business, the company purchased North American rights to a complicated device for making finely detailed **animal crackers**. Saint John's Great Fire destroyed their buildings but within a month T. Rankine Sons Limited had set up ovens inside a tent and in less than a year had constructed a new plant. Thomas Rankine was also active in local affairs, serving as one of the first directors of the Saint John Mechanics Institute. He died in 1871 but his family continued to operate the business until after World War II.

Early Apple Industry

By 1610, cultivated **apple orchards** had been planted in North America at Port Royal using Normandy apples. Early French apple varieties were mainly developed for cider so that table-use apples were largely selected and cultivated by the later Loyalists and New England Planters. One such Planter was Charles Ramage Prescott of Starrs Point in the Annapolis Valley. He introduced over one hundred apple varieties into the Maritimes, including the most popular local apple the **Gravenstein**.

In London, Prescott acquired scions of what had originally been German apples and brought them to Nova Scotia as green ripening yellow apples. Prescott's interest in experimental fruit horticulture caused him to freely distribute his scions throughout the Valley. A popular red-streaked variety of Gravenstein was discovered in 1876 at Waterville and later a full red variety became known as Crimson Gravenstein.

As a highly versatile early apple, capable of being grown only in a few places worldwide, the Gravenstein quickly became the provincial favourite, as well as a popular export apple for both cooking and eating fresh. Annapolis Valley apples were the first **Canadian fruit** to be commercially exported, mainly to Britain and the West Indies beginning about 1820.

Charles Prescott established what many consider the first **experimental farm** in the region at his Acadia Grove manor, promoting fruit grafting, hot-houses, and other agricultural innovations, including the cultivation of many exotic fruits and vegetables. Bough Sweet and the Northern Spy are among the many other commercial varieties of apples Prescott introduced into Nova Scotia. He died in 1859 and his Prescott House home is now a fully restored museum.

An early **modern horticulturalist** in Canada and one of the first in North America to hybridize apple and pears, was Francis Peabody Sharp of Upper Woodstock, New Brunswick. Born in 1823, Sharp moved to Upper Woodstock in 1844 and established one of the earliest family apple orchards in New Brunswick as well as the first significant experimental fruit nursery. For almost a hundred years, virtually all grafted varieties of apples in the province came from his nurseries as apples became an important export industry for New Brunswick. Considered the father of fruit culture in New Brunswick, Sharp developed or discovered many new apple varieties including one in 1853 called New Brunswick, and his most famous apple **Crimson Beauty** which he originally called Early Scarlet.

Chocolates and The First Chocolate Bar

Chocolates were first produced in Canada in 1844 by John Mott of John P. Mott & Co. of Dartmouth who had acquired the knowledge of chocolate making from the first American chocolate producers, Walter Baker Co. of Dorchester, Massachusetts. The Dartmouth Chocolate Works had been established almost ten years earlier by John's father, Henry Mott, with assistance from the Nova Scotia Legislature as he began importing cheap sugar from the West Indies.

Little however was known about the candy-making process, until Mott's daughter married into the Baker family and the Motts acquired technical assistance from the Massachusetts chocolate company. The Canadian pio-

1871 advertisement for food manufacturer John P. Mott, whose company established Canada's earliest chocolate works. While their retail office was in Halifax, the manufacturing mill was in Dartmouth overlooking Halifax harbour.

neer chocolate maker continued to operate until 1920 when the last remaining partner passed away. John Mott himself also owned a soap-making business and was involved in a number of successful Nova Scotian enterprises before dying in 1890.

The most famous chocolate company in Canada, Ganong Bros. Ltd. of St. Stephen, New Brunswick, invented the world's first **chocolate nut bar** in 1910, when Arthur Ganong and candy-maker George Ensor decided to produce milk chocolate from the family's Jersey cow and moulded it with nuts into narrow pieces. The results were delightful and became a convenient snack for customers to take on fishing trips. The five-cent bar became popular and the chocolate business expanded rapidly outperforming the family bakery, as well as their soap factory with its popular Surprise Soap.

James and Gilbert Ganong established the candy company in 1873, the same year their chief Maritime chocolate rival the Moirs Company of Halifax began business. But unlike the fiercely independent Ganongs, and despite having the best selling box of chocolates in Canada, the Pot of Gold, Moirs became part of the American-owned Hershey Foods Ltd. The Ganongs managed to maintain ownership and as innovators continued to strive to improve their confectionery products and earned a reputation for excellence in the chocolate industry.

The company was among the first in Canada to use the newly developed **plastic materials** when in 1889 it patented a process of using celluloid pads for imprinting their letters GB on the bottom of individual chocolates. Early marketing initiatives also succeeded as they promoted their products with the marketing slogan "The Maker's Mark On Every Piece." Ganong Bros. also became the first in Canada to put **nuts in sweet chocolate**, as well as to make **lollipops, valentine-shaped candy boxes**, and to wrap bars and boxes in **cellophane**.

They also pioneered the packaged **miniature chocolates**, the **All-Day Sucker**, and the Maritime favourite, the **Chicken Bone**. Ganong's became famous for its hand-dipped chocolates where an experienced employee could dip up to twelve thousand chocolates a day. During the 1930s and the cod-liver oil craze, the company even developed a cod liver oil chocolate bar. Today the Ganong company is the only family owned, large candy company in Canada, and still maintains a factory and company headquarters in St. Stephen.

Reindeer Condensed Milk

The first dairy in Canada to produce **condensed milk** was the Truro Condensed Milk and Canning Company. Condensed milk, coffee and cocoa were produced under the Reindeer brand in a wooden, two-storey factory with fifteen employees. The condensed products began to appear in 1883 and proved popular with consumers once the company guaranteed their safety and purity by having a doctor, David Muir, who also happened to be mayor of Truro, serve as the company's president. Muir was also a member of the Nova Scotia provincial medical board and a graduate of the New York College of Physicians and Surgeons.

The dairy promoted the new condensed milk as "endorsed by the medical faculty" and assured consumers they were guaranteed a "good, pure, and healthy article." In 1884, the company reported canning two hundred thousand cans of milk and also produced canned fruit. They exhibited their condensed products worldwide, winning first prizes at Antwerp and London food fairs.

Red Rose Tea

While the Maritime enterprise of J.E. Morse and Company is considered Canada's **oldest tea firm**, Red Rose Tea is certainly its most famous variety. Despite earning merely $166 in tea sales during his first year in business, Saint John merchant Theodore Estabrooks decided to concentrate his tiny Dock Street enterprise on importing tea products. Estabrooks had an idea he was convinced would work — produce a high grade tea that always tasted consistent and sell it in an attractive package.

Before 1900, Canadians drank Chinese, Japanese, or East Indian tea sold in bulk, which often varied in taste despite sometimes coming from the same plantation. Estabrooks was convinced that tea from India and Ceylon was superior and soon began experimenting in his Saint John shop, blending and packaging various mixtures. He convinced the Indian tea agent, W. R. Miles, whose family had been professional tea-tasters in Britain, to join him as his tea-taster to ensure uniform taste and quality.

Forming the T.H. Estabrooks Company, Estabrooks chose **Red Rose** as his trade name and adopted the advertising slogan "Red Rose tea is good tea." That simple yet exceptional advertising statement so assured consumers that Red Rose tea was indeed superior quality tea, that soon tremendous quantities of tea were being sold throughout Canada and abroad.

Estabrooks managed to maintain uniform taste by always blending tea from at least three different plantations. The company even packaged different sizes, including the half ounce pack for the West Indies. By 1900, Estabrooks annual turnover of tea had surpassed almost one million kilograms (2 million pounds) and eventually became the **largest tea and coffee company** in Canada with a large tea blending, packing and shipping plant on Saint John's North Wharf.

The first **tea bag machine** in Canada was reportedly installed at Estabrooks' plant by its inventor, an American named Dalton, who had come up with the device by tinkering with a cigarette-making machine. The company began offering Red Rose coffee for sale about 1910 and while the product proved popular, it didn't achieve the same demand as its tea. In 1932, Estabrooks sold control of his company to British interests yet today, Red Rose Tea is still consumed by many Canadians.

Canned Salmon Factory

In 1839, Tristram Halliday established Canada's first commercial **salmon canning factory** on the Bay of Fundy, near Saint John. During the same period Halliday, with American partners the Treat Company, was also involved in setting up salmon and lobster canneries in Maine, especially around Eastport. While Halliday was the first to preserve salmon in sealed tins, the required method of preparation was still not properly understood since his first finished products were disappointing. The canning appliances were crude, including the soldered lids, and the quality of cans inferior, often causing the cans to puncture or burst.

The process of hermetically sealing perishable food in tin containers was first developed successfully by John Moir and Son of Aberdeen, Scotland about 1821. The complicated process involved boiling the food inside the sealed can, venting the tin and resealing the containers. A Scottish tinsmith, Charles Mitchell, brought the new technology to Canada, and while residing in Halifax, began exporting canned food to Britain from Canada.

Halliday and his partners attempted unsuccessfully to acquire the patent for Mitchell's airtight canning method. In 1843 they finally secured his services and began expanding their improved canned lobster and salmon operations, exporting their products and opening new canneries.

Oldest Fish Company

Lunenburg was established in 1753 as the second British colonial settlement in Nova Scotia after Halifax and in 1789, John Zwicker founded Zwicker and Company, the **oldest fish company** in Canada. During the nineteenth century, the company became very active in the West Indies trade, exporting fish products to the Caribbean in exchange for sugar, rum, molasses and other foods. A successor, William N. Zwicker, has been described as the leading West Indies merchant in Lunenburg. At one point, Zwicker's was the only Lunenburg company with sailing vessels regularly shipping to the West Indies.

William N. Zwicker also pioneered the deep sea fishing expeditions that established Lunenburg's fishing reputation, when, in 1859, he sent the schooner *Union* to the Grand Banks off Newfoundland. Twenty years later, Lunenburg's Captain Benjamin Anderson began the extremely profitable but dangerous practice of **deep sea trawlfishing** from dories, as his schooner *Dylitris* began making regular trips to the Grand Banks. Fishing with multiple baited hooks on a single line from small boats revolutionized the fishing industry, with Lunenburg becoming the fishing capital of Canada's East Coast.

From the company's headquarters at 152 Montague Street, Zwicker and Company remained one of the most active fish merchants in Nova Scotia for almost two hundred years. The business remained in the Zwicker family until 1977 when it was sold to Lunenburg-based fishing company Deep Sea Trawlers Ltd.

Salmon Hatchery

The first Canadian **fish hatchery** that successfully bred salmon was established by Samuel Wilmot in 1873 on the Northwest Miramichi River at the mouth of Stewart Brook. A number of European countries claim credit for first having hatched fish eggs, including Germany where a man named Jacobi is reported to have artificially fertilized trout eggs well before 1800. What is known about the fish breeding process is that by 1850 a salmon hatchery was installed on the River Tay in Scotland and in Norway the same year.

In 1866 Wilmot erected Canada's first fish culture station on Lake Ontario. An eminent pisciculturist and the originator of Canadian aquaculture, Wilmot mainly raised trout at his Lake Ontario hatchery. He did manage to spawn some salmon eggs, although he failed in his attempt to re-establish salmon in Ontario.

A member of the prominent Wilmot family of New Brunswick Loyalists, Samuel Wilmot was sent to the Miramichi by Newcastle politician and Father of Confederation Peter Mitchell. As the first Federal Minister of Marine and Fisheries, Mitchell showed keen interest in increasing the salmon fishery. Even by the 1860s, the Atlantic Salmon population had decreased in numbers due to extensive net fishing, poaching, as well as construction of sawmills and other industrial developments.

Wilmot chose the Stewart River site about eight kilometres (5 miles) upriver from Newcastle because of its continual supply of clean water. With local assistance he built a fish breeding station and began releasing salmon eggs into the various Miramichi River streams. The next year, Issac Sheasgreen became fish hatchery supervisor as the operation began releasing six hundred thousand young salmon annually, quickly increasing the salmon population throughout the Miramichi River system.

Wilmot developed innovative hatchery techniques and designs that were widely copied. Under Mitchell's ministry he became manager of the entire hatchery system throughout Canada. Despite establishment of many more salmon breeding stations, the Stewart Brook hatchery remained in operation for well over one hundred years.

Frozen Fish Fillets

An American, Clarence Birdseye, is usually considered the founder of the frozen food industry but Dr. Archibald G. Huntsman actually pioneered the frozen fish process. In 1926, while director of the Halifax Fisheries Experimental Station, which later became part of the Fisheries Research Board of Canada, Huntsman began to develop his frozen fish, called "**Ice Fillets.**" They contained packaged, fast-frozen fish fillets. About forty-five metric tons (50 tons) were sold throughout Canada during 1929, especially in the Toronto area, by the Board and two Nova Scotia fish companies, Lunenburg Sea Products Co. and Lockeport Co.

Huntsman had become the first in North America to freeze food commercially and to market frozen fish fillets. He demonstrated that the freezing process worked well for fishery products and that its commercial viability was not in doubt. For over two years, Ice Fillets were supplied to the Toronto market and demand exceeded supply, despite high retail pricing.

The Atlantic fishing industry did not develop his processing innovation, partly because fresh fish dealers were opposed to the idea. By 1931, the fisheries scientist's demonstration had been terminated. Clarence Birdseye, who had developed the process independently of Huntsman, acquired financial help to launch his line of frozen foods and achieved commercial success in the United States.

Huntsman's theories about Atlantic Salmon were controversial and later largely disproved, but his technical innovations in fisheries research were unsurpassed. He invented the **jacketed cold storage principle** in order to improve frozen and smoked seafood products. At the Halifax station he constructed a cold storage room and built a jacket of refrigerating pipes that circulated cold air around the storage room instead of inside it. Huntsman was able to improve the quality of the frozen fish by reducing the dehydration or drying-out effect. This refrigeration method was clearly superior to other cold storage methods, but again the fishing industry ignored Huntsman's accomplishment and did not adopt the innovation for another twenty-five years.

Archibald Huntsman devoted his life to fisheries research and continued to combine experimental work with teaching, writing, and consulting about marine science, especially on problems of salmon management. He died at St. Andrews, in 1973, after establishing the Huntsman Marine Fisheries Station.

Marine Science

St. Andrews, situated at the head of Passamaquoddy Bay in the Bay of Fundy, is surrounded by one of the most productive marine life areas along the entire east coast. In 1898, Canada's first **biological station** began at nearby Indian Point, when a small group of marine scientists built a mobile floating laboratory described as being similar to an ark-like streetcar mounted on a barge. Operational until 1906, the floating station also spent time at Canso, Gaspé and Malpeque.

The station was established by the federal government who had created a special management board, the Biological Board of Canada, to oversee the operation. Later, in 1908, it constructed a permanent, on-shore fisheries research station. The Fisheries Research Board's St. Andrews station has had an enormous influence on the fishery in the Bay of Fundy and has led to creation of the Passamaquoddy Bay area as the leading aquaculture centre in eastern Canada, especially in relation to salmon farming.

Canada's largest federal **research centre for oceanography** and now one of the three largest marine science centres in the western hemisphere, was established in 1962 on the shores of Halifax harbour's Bedford Basin. The Bedford Institute of Oceanography conducts oceanographic studies and hydrographic surveys, as well as navigational, energy and fisheries research in the marine environments of the Atlantic and Arctic oceans.

In 1970, as part of its marine research, the Bedford Institute's vessel, the *CSS Hudson* became the first ship to **circumnavigate the Americas**. During an eleven-month voyage to four oceans around South and North America, the 4,264 metric ton (4,700 ton) *Hudson* carried over one hundred staff from the international scientific community and conducted a variety of marine studies and experiments.

Other important innovations involving the Bedford Institute include the remotely-operated, electric undersea vehicle, the **Deep Rover**, one of the most advanced one-person submarines ever developed. Built by Can-Dive in Dartmouth, the underwater sea buggy can descend to one thousand metres (3,280 feet) in depth and can remain underwater for up to one week. Used extensively for marine science and undersea construction, *Deep Rover* has also been used for oil exploration on the continental shelf and was initially developed specifically to monitor the remaining oil in the controversial sunken barge, *Irving Whale*, now lying off the coast of Prince Edward Island.

An underwater towed vehicle called the **Batfish**, while built at Fathom Oceanology in Ontario, was designed at the Bedford Institute in Dartmouth. Towed behind a ship, the *Batfish* operates like a tiny airplane zooming up and down underwater, gathering information and collecting plankton samples. The 1.4 metre (4-½ foot) device is also equipped to transport marine research instrument packages to aid in oceanographic research.

Factory Freezer Trawler

The earliest **factory freezer trawler** to operate in Canadian waters was the *Fairtry*, launched out of England in 1953. In November 1985, Canada's largest fish processing company, National Sea Products Ltd. of Lunenburg, was granted a trawler licence and within two months was operating Canada's first real factory freezer trawler. Named the *Cape North*, it was purchased from the West German Pickenpack fishing group and licensed to fish non-traditional species in Canada's east coast waters.

The steel-hulled, eighty-two metre (270 foot) -long trawler was the fifty-eighth vessel in National Sea's deep-sea fleet but unique inside with its modern conveyor belts, mechanical boners, headers and gutters, and filleting operators, allowing for instant freezing of freshly caught fish. Capable of storing up to 671 metric tons (740 tons) of frozen fish product, the *Cape North* became the controversial symbol of Canada's fishing expansion efforts of the late 1970s and 1980s. Due to reduced fishing quotas, National Sea sold the *Cape North* in early 1994.

Spud Island

The first **seed potatoes** developed in Canada were shipped from Prince Edward Island to Ontario in 1918. The potatoes were of the Irish Cobbler variety, and had been certified free of viral diseases two years earlier. The Island's potato industry quickly developed into a significant agricultural commodity with annual exports worldwide. Besides the important seed potato market, which established the industry's high quality reputation, each year important quantities of table potatoes are also shipped off Island.

Scottish Malt Whiskey Distillery

At Glenville in the Highlands of Cape Breton, the first **single malt distillery** in North America was established in 1991. Glenora Distillery, one of only two single malt distilleries outside Scotland, acquired the malt whiskey recipe from Scotland and began bottling the Scotch the same year. To acquire the unique malt flavour, the whiskey is aged in wooden casks for at least five years. Tours of the distillery are given throughout the summer months and Glenora is now a popular tourist destination in Cape Breton.

Energy and Mining

"Of all the substances ever taken from the earth, coal is certainly the most useful. Coal is power . . ." —Abraham Gesner, prior to his invention of kerosene, *Remarks on the Geology and Mineralogy of Nova Scotia*, 1836.

Coal Mining

Coal was reported to have been first mined in North America in 1643 at Grand Lake, New Brunswick, when Charles La Tour sailed up the Saint John River to the north side of Grand Lake, near Minto, and loaded coal for Boston. This small, open pit mine was later operated for the export trade and an historic monument has been erected at Minto to commemorate the beginning of coal mining in North America. Samuel Pepys, the famous 1660s English diarist, makes reference to the site as the only known place for mining coal in America.

Coal mining in Canada as an industry first began in Cape Breton where coal had been noted along the coastal cliffs as early as Nicolas Denys' 1672 published journals. The earliest extensive **commercial coal mining** in Canada began in 1720 at Port Morien, Cape Breton, to supply fuel to Louisbourg, which became one of the largest military centres in North America. By the mid-1800s, most of Canada's coal was supplied from Cape Breton, making the island one of the most prosperous areas in the region.

The Cape Breton coal mines extend far underground, out beneath the sea, and millions of tons have been exported or burned within Canada since 1720. The Phalen seam at Dominion No. 2 was developed in 1899 and was tapped at 165 metres (541 feet) while the shaft, at twelve metres by 3.5 metres (39 by 11 feet), was considered North America's **largest**.

Glace Bay miners in 1906 were the first in North America to wear the self-contained **breathing apparatus** in mine rescue work. Made in Europe, the oxygen breathing apparatus was built around an air tank, and began to appear in British coal mines around 1870. The ability to breathe and work in gas greatly increased the mine rescue corps' effectiveness.

The first major **coal mine disaster** in Canada occurred in Pictou County where more than six hundred men have died producing approximately sixty million metric tons (55 million tons) of coal. The first reported deaths due to gas explosions occurred in 1838 at the General Mining Association Store Pit # 2 when two boys, William Lowe and James Conn, announced that their safety lamps indicated a heavy build-up of gas nine metres (30 feet) into the shaft. An explosion blew the young men out of the pit, killing them instantly. A coroner's inquest ruled the disaster "accidental death by explosion of gas."

In 1873, a methane explosion killed sixty men and boys at the Westville Drummond Mine, operated by the Intercolonial Coal Company. Opened in 1868 as part of the Acadia coal seam, annual production peaked in just four years, but like most Pictou County coal mines, Drummond became dangerous due to combustible gas build-ups. An inquiry placed part of the blame for the original underground fire on the use of blasting powder. The Drummond Mine finally closed in 1984 due to declining reserves. Just six years earlier, the last pit pony in North America was reportedly led out of the shaft.

Electricity From Coal

The inventor of electricity, Thomas Edison, had long considered transporting coal by rail from mines to factories an unnecessary expense and advocated establishing power plants at the mine shafts and transporting the energy by wire to consumers. A published interview with Edison convinced directors of the Maritime Coal, Railway and Power Company, operators of the Chignecto Coal Mines near Maccan in Cumberland County, Nova Scotia, to seriously look at Edison's idea of pit-mouth coal generation.

After visiting Edison in the United States, the company's president, Senator William Mitchell decided to build a coal-electric power plant at the mouth of the Chignecto mine. On July 31, 1907, the Lieutenant Governor of Nova Scotia, D. C. Fraser, pulled a switch to produce electricity from the first **pit-mouth coal power plant** in North America.

Edison's father had been born in Digby and his interest in the project was such that he sent a congratulatory telegram to the company. With plenty of coal and convinced that costs compared favourably with hydro development, Maritime coal companies began to produce thermal electricity. Using Edison's idea, and the Maritime Coal Company's example, the new power plants were all built near mine sites in order to avoid heavy transportation costs.

Abraham Gesner's Kerosene

Abraham Gesner invented kerosene and began extracting it from albertite coal in 1846 at Albert County, New Brunswick. He demonstrated the burning fluid as superior lamp oil the same year during a public exhibition at the Mechanics Institute in Charlottetown. Born in the Annapolis Valley, Gesner trained as a physician but became interested in geology. In 1837 he became Canada's first **Provincial Geologist** for New Brunswick.

A founder of the petroleum industry, Gesner succeed in distilling his fuel from solid hydrocarbons and termed the product kerosene, intended as a replacement fuel for the whale-oil lamps that produced uneven light. Gesner's process of extracting kerosene from hydrocarbons by low temperature distillation was a scientific breakthrough of international significance. The new fuel was first **used commercially** in a lighthouse at McNab's Island in Halifax harbour. With banker Enos Collins' financial support, Gesner established the Kerosene Gas Light Company and attempted to market his new fuel.

Gesner obtained a US patent for his invention after failing to secure local rights and in 1854 moved to Long Island, New York, where he established a company to manufacture kerosene from asphalt. He published the first **textbook** on the new lighting fuel, *A Practical Treatise on Coal, Petroleum, and other Distilled Oils*. At age sixty-five, having sold his US company to Rockefeller's Standard Oil, Gesner returned to Halifax less than a wealthy man. The discovery of natural oil rendered his fuel too expensive for widespread use.

In 1863 Gesner became professor of Natural History at Dalhousie University but poor health plagued his teaching career. Gesner's invention was the precursor of all modern petroleum fuels and transformed nine-

Abraham Gesner, the inventor of kerosene and the founder of Canada's first public museum. (Public Archives of Nova Scotia)

teenth-century life by providing safe, bright lighting to all. Kerosene was used extensively until petroleum became widely available. Imperial Oil erected a monument to this Maritime inventor at his grave site in the Camp Hill Cemetery at Halifax. Although wealthy at times, Abraham Gesner suffered from financial problems most of his life, but did become one of the few Maritime inventors who received recognition for his achievements during his lifetime.

Oil Spill Disaster

The first **bulk cargo of oil** shipped to a Canadian port entered Halifax in 1899 aboard the steamer *Maverick*.

The first major Canadian **oil spill at sea** occurred in 1970 in Chedabucto Bay, Nova Scotia, when the 9,979 metric ton (11,000 ton) Liberian tanker *Arrow* ran aground on Cerberus Rock. Oil polluted almost two hundred kilometres (125 miles) of Nova Scotia shoreline and almost nine million litres

(2 million gallons) of the bunker oil escaped into the Strait of Canso. Despite nearly half the oil being recovered, the spill caused serious destruction to marine and bird life. The oil was recovered by means of four "slicklickers," invented by chemist Richard Sewell in order to soak up huge quantities of surface oil for re-use. Despite heavy seas in Chedabucto Bay, the cleanup was somewhat successful.

Tidal Power

The first commercial use of **tidal power** in North America undoubtedly had to do with sawing lumber and grinding grain. These tidal mills reportedly had been established throughout the reaches of the giant Bay of Fundy tides from the time of the arrival of Europeans up to the late nineteenth century.

The only **tidal electrical power plant** in North America opened at Annapolis Royal in 1984 as a pilot project to demonstrate the feasibility of electrical generation from the Fundy tides. The plant employs the largest turbine ever built for hydroelectric development, a Straflo or prototype straight-flow turbine, and produces about fifty million kilowatt-hours annually for the Nova Scotia Power Company.

In order to produce electric power, the ebb and flow of the tides are controlled by means of a dam at the plant's site near the mouth of the Annapolis River. Although the efficiency of the turbine for tidal power production has been established, questions concerning costs and environmental considerations, especially fish kill, make any large-scale expansion of tidal power projects uncertain.

Heavy Water

The world's first commercial **heavy water plant** opened in 1967 by Nova Scotia Premier Robert Stanfield at Glace Bay. Deuterium of Canada Ltd. built the Glace Bay plant to produce heavy water from sea water for use in developing electrical power through nuclear energy by controlling the fission of the uranium in the reactor. Major corrosion problems held back actual production and a second plant at Point Tupper, Nova Scotia, developed by Canadian General Electric, actually produced the first heavy water. Both plants were closed in the 1980s due to lack of demand for the water.

Offshore Oil

After thirty years of exploration, at 8:00 A.M. on June 5, 1992, production of Canada's first **offshore oil** began at the Cohasset-Panuke oil fields about forty kilometres (25 miles) southwest of Sable Island on the Scotian Shelf. The initial sweet crude, known as Scotian Light, came from the Panuke fields and was of exceptionally high quality with low sulphur content. The premium crude was purchased at just under $22 US a barrel and shipped to a US refinery along the Gulf of Mexico. In the same year, the Maritimes only major oil company, Irving Oil Ltd. began refining the crude at its Saint John facility, the **largest refinery** in Canada. Production was undertaken jointly on a fifty–fifty basis by the operator, LASMO Nova Scotia Ltd a subsidiary of British multinational Lasmo PLC, and Nova Scotia Resources Ltd. a provincial Crown corporation.

Production facilities for these off shore oil wells are located on a jack-up rig where oil is pumped to the surface, transferred to a storage tanker moored to a monobuoy and shipped to shore by a shuttle tanker called *Nordic Challenger*. The oil was drilled by the *Rowan Gorilla III* rig which also served as the project's production rig. By 1994, production reached twelve thousand barrels a day earning $30 to $40 million per year in profits. Despite significant oil reserves, estimated at fifty million barrels, a huge debt from drilling and production cost overruns make further expansion of the resource doubtful.

The first Canadian built **semisubmersible oil rig** was constructed during the 1980s at Saint John by the Saint John Shipbuilding & Dry Dock Company Ltd. Also built by the Irving Group of Saint John was Canaport, the first **deep-water port** in Canada specifically designed for supertankers.

Health and Medicine

"Notice is hereby given to the Publick that they may be attended during any disorder by a regular bred surgeon and apothecary, with advice gratis, with medicines at the same rate as in England, and without any charge for visits, unless sent for after the nine o'clock gun firing. Likewise all persons under necessity of employing a man midwife, may be served by

Their most humble servant

Henry Meriton"

— First newspaper advertisement by a doctor in Canada. *Halifax Gazette* July 21, 1753.

Aboriginal Medicine

Prior to white contact, over five hundred years ago, the Mi'kmaq and Maliseet people of the Maritimes relied on **natural medicines** derived from plants, trees, and animal parts to cure sickness and accelerate healing. Aches and pains, as well as external injuries from accidents, were treated with herbal remedies. More serious emotional or internal illnesses were usually dealt with by shamans or spirit-helpers as these misfortunes were considered the result of weak spiritual powers. Attempting to restore the missing spiritual knowledge, these respected members of the native community would perform elaborate healing rituals.

But traditional native lifestyles incorporated good dietary practices and exhibited little serious sickness before the introduction of **European diseases**. Nicolas Denys describes the Mi'kmaq he found on Cape Breton in his 1672 book, *Geographical Description of the Coasts of North America*: "If any accident happened to them . . ., they did not need a physician. They had knowledge of herbs, of which they made use and straightway grew well."

With little immunity to the simple cold virus as well as smallpox, typhoid and other diseases brought from Europe, native communities became infected *en masse*. It is estimated that diseases wiped out up to seventy-five per cent of the Maritime aboriginal population after only a hundred years of contact. The Mi'kmaq communities of the coastal Maritimes were among the first North American natives to encounter the Europeans and, with no natural immunity to the white man's illnesses, were particularly hard hit by a whole range of strange new diseases. Their traditional remedies proved ineffective and the ensuing collision between the two cultures devastated the native people.

Doctor Louis Hébert

In the era of European exploration, French law insisted that all ships leaving France carry a surgeon. While also the ship's barber and often the cook's helper, surgeons provided many essential services. We know that Surgeon Ripault sailed with Jacques Cartier and both Columbus and Cabot had health officers aboard.

While Deschamps de Honfleur performed a post-mortem on a French scurvy victim at St. Croix in 1605, and Surgeon Estienne was active the same year at Port Royal, the first real **European doctor** to practise in North America was apothecary Louis Hébert. Born in Paris, Hébert arrived at Port Royal in July of 1606 with his cousin Poutrincourt. He visited North America three times before becoming a permanent resident at Quebec in 1617. His 1610 voyage from France to Port Royal included his wife Marie Hébert, the first known **white female resident** in Canada. Knowledgeable in many fields, including horticulture, Hébert is also considered the earliest **European farmer** and first **Officer of Justice**. Both activities were undertaken at Port Royal, where he was reported to have been paid 100 livres a year for his services.

Hébert's most important asset to the struggling settlement was his knowledge of the medicinal properties of herbs and other plants. Besides growing and administering his herbal remedies, Hébert is said to have used local clay to produce a plaster for fellow settler Robert Gravé's damaged hand. Hébert treated both French and Indian patients and was reportedly on excellent terms with the local Mi'kmaq community, with whom he exchanged information on herbal medicine. After his return to Port Royal,

Hébert administered to the dying Mi'kmaq chief Henri Membertou in 1611. He died at Quebec in 1627 after falling on the ice.

Oldest Drug Store

In 1810 Thomas Desbrisay Jr. opened Apothecaries' Hall, the **oldest working drugstore** in Canada, in Charlottetown at the corner of Grafton and Queen. The pharmacy remained in operation at the same location, dispensing medicine and giving medical advice for 175 years. Desbrisay and his son Theophilus ran the drugstore business until 1874 when George Hughes and his partner, Dr. Frank Beer, acquired it. At the turn of the century, a new brick building was constructed at the same location across from Confederation Centre and George Hughes and his Hughes Drug Company gained full ownership of Apothecaries's Hall.

Drugs and druggists remained unregulated throughout the nineteenth century on Prince Edward Island and most patented medicines contained morphine, opium or alcohol. Despite doctors' attempts to gain control of pharmacists' prescriptions, it was well into this century before the Prince Edward Island Medical Society was able to convince legislators to limit the unrestricted use of patent medicines.

Doctor Parker and Anesthesia

Daniel McNeill Parker was born in 1822 and began his career at the Asylum for the Poor in Halifax. There, in 1847, he became the first physician in Canada to operate with the assistance of the **anesthetic ether**. Parker received his medical training under the Halifax physician William Bruce Almon and also studied medicine at the University of Edinburgh, winning the gold medal in anatomy. He returned to Halifax and began working as a surgeon. After a patient escaped the operating table in mid-operation, Parker began to search for a sedative other than brandy. Prior to the use of anesthesia, patients were often given alcohol and strapped in place or held down by assistants during protracted operations.

Parker first learned of Dr. William Morton's successful use of sulphuric ether in an operation at the Massachusetts General Hospital in Boston through Halifax dentist Lawrence E. Van Buskirk, who had witnessed its administration. Early in 1847, Van Buskirk administered ether to Parker

Daniel McNeill Parker, first physician in Canada to operate with the assistance of anesthesia. (Public Archives of Nova Scotia)

experimentally and the following day, Parker became the first Canadian physician to operate with the help of anesthesia. Van Buskirk reportedly administered the ether to the patient, while Parker amputated the woman's leg.

Often cited as an important medical advancement due to the reduction of pain, the introduction of anesthesia during medical procedures also occurred the same year in New Brunswick. Doctor Martin H. Peters became the first **physician** in New Brunswick to use ether during surgery when he removed a tumor from a patient's arm in a Saint John hospital. A Saint John dental surgeon, Dr. Fiske, administered the ether.

Parker continued to do medical research and travelled to Europe in 1871 to further study his specialty antiseptic surgery. Interested in improving medical practices in Victorian Halifax, he was present in the operating theatre when William J. Almon became the first doctor in Canada to use chloroform on a patient during surgery. Parker had wide business interests but practised medicine in Halifax for over fifty years and founded the Medical Society of Nova Scotia. He also assisted in creation of the Medical Faculty at Dalhousie University, and served as president of the Canadian Medical Association. He was a driving force behind establishment of the largest public hospital in Nova Scotia, the Victoria General.

Chloroform and the Pictou Chemist

In 1848, Pictou druggist and entrepreneur J.D.B. Fraser became the first druggist in Canada to manufacture and administer **chloroform** as an anesthetic, giving it to his wife during the birth of their child, Robert Peter Fraser. Chemist Fraser produced the chloroform from a formula he found published in a British medical journal written by Sir James Young Simpson, the first physician in Britain to demonstrate its effective use as an anesthetic. Fraser succeeded in preparing and purifying the substance at his Pictou drug store on Water Street, just four months after Simpson first used the anesthetic in Scotland.

During the late 1840s, religious controversy surrounded the use of chloroform, especially in assisting childbirth, since the Bible in Genesis III stated: "In pain you shall bring forth children." Fraser attempted to reassure people by giving a public demonstration on chloroform and its properties before the Pictou Literary and Scientific Society in 1848. But it was not until Queen Victoria used chloroform in 1853 in assisting the birth of her seventh child, Prince Leopold, that its use became widely accepted.

Fraser also began to supply Halifax doctors with the anesthetic, initially to Dr. William James Almon who became the first doctor in Canada to **use chloroform in a hospital** on February 5, 1848. Almon amputated a woman's thumb at the City Almshouse on Doyle Street and a month later also amputated a patient's limb with the assistance of the substance. Chloroform was administered by inhaling from a rag applied to the nose and mouth of the patient.

James Daniel Bain Fraser was more than a leading pioneer in Canadian pharmacology. He was also a businessman in Pictou County with many interests. Besides co-founding modern marine salvage in Canada, Fraser owned three drugstores in Pictou, was stagecoach agent for the Pictou to Halifax line, ran a stone quarry that shipped grindstones to Boston and became involved in the local coal mining industry.

Fraser also experimented with charcoal and in 1850 exhibited an **electric light** fuelled by the burning of charcoal with an electrical current. This was an important innovation since it was not until about 1860 that the principle of the electric light, complete with a carbon filament, had been fully refined.

Mental Asylum

While the Hôtel-Dieu hospital in Quebec had provided a ward for mentally ill women as early as 1714, New Brunswick became the first province to provide separate **mental facilities** when the asylum for the mentally ill was opened in 1836 on Leinster Street in Saint John. The previous year, two dozen reputed mentally ill patients had been imprisoned in the county jail, then moved to the city's almshouse, and finally assigned to the basement of the Leinster Street cholera hospital.

Saint John was experiencing high levels of immigration during the 1830s and began building a number of institutions to deal with the social crisis of receiving boatloads of immigrants. The mentally ill were either judged as criminals or sent to the poor asylum, although those who could afford treatment were sent to Britain or the United States.

Dr. George Peters, medical officer at the city's jail and almshouse, led the move to segregate the insane from criminals and the physically sick. Born in Saint John but educated in Scotland, Peters knew of the European view developed in the early 1800s that mental illness was curable through humane treatment.

Horrified to find the mentally ill incarcerated in jails, many under heavy restraint, often naked and filthy, Peters convinced the Saint John authorities to move the insane to the separate asylum in the basement of the cholera hospital. He was paid £100 a year as superintendent and immediately began to petition for a permanent asylum. Twelve years later, in 1848, a permanent treatment centre, called the Provincial Lunatic Asylum, opened near the Reversing Falls.

The asylum's first superintendent was Dr. John Waddell, who immediately began to petition for an addition to the institution, claiming the centre was inadequate. By 1864, the asylum housed almost two hundred patients as the concept of mental illness as a disease needing treatment became firmly established in Canada. Saint John's asylum was also apparently responsible for making Houdini famous. A story in Dr. W. Brenton Stewart's *Medicine In New Brunswick* relates that in 1896 the famous escape artist got his first **straitjacket** and the idea for his escape routine while visiting the facility.

Quarantine Station

As called for in Saint John's Royal Charter, the first official **quarantine station** in Canada was established in 1785 at Partridge Island in Saint John harbour. Halifax, Montreal and Quebec had for many years make-shift holding areas for incoming sick immigrants. But in laying out Saint John, the Royal Charter called for a designated quarantine location and pest house, away from the populated community.

Contagious diseases were known at the time to be transported by ships and epidemics, including smallpox, typhus, cholera and influenza, were common, often affecting whole communities. Smallpox was particularly widespread in the late 1700s and incoming vessels with sick aboard were required to fly a yellow flag in the starboard rigging. Quarantine periods on the island often lasted one to two months.

Partridge Island's first inspection station was actually erected in 1830 due to the widespread fear of a cholera epidemic. Immigrants landing at Saint John were mainly from Ireland or Britain, with over sixty per cent of the more than two thousand bodies buried on the island in mass graves considered to be of Irish descent. The year 1847 was particularly difficult as well over six hundred immigrants were buried at Partridge Island, victims of typhus.

Doctors treating the victims were also affected as was the chief health officer, Dr. George Harding and his brother William. Both survived but a young Irish volunteer, Dr. James Patrick Collins, died at age twenty-three, a victim of typhus. George Harding continued to serve as Partridge Island's medical doctor for forty years.

In 1974, Partridge Island was designated a National Historic Site for its role as a quarantine station. Two celtic crosses, one in Saint John and the other on the island itself, stand as memorials to the thousands of immigrants who crossed the Atlantic, attempting to escape famine and disease.

First Health Department

Dr. William F. Roberts, New Brunswick's Minister Without Portfolio in Walter Foster's Liberal government, in 1918 established the first separate **Department of Public Health** in Canada. Previously public health had been usually considered the responsibility of the Agriculture Department where the deputy minister was often a doctor. The Saint John doctor established the new department after becoming alarmed by an influenza epidemic called the Spanish flu that came into Canada with returning World War I troops.

As minister in charge, Roberts immediately prohibited for five weeks all gathering of over five people in New Brunswick, closing schools, churches, and other public meeting sites. While the influenza eventually killed thousands of Canadians, Roberts' action was credited with saving lives in New Brunswick. William Roberts however was also a controversial figure.

Concerned about infant mortality, Roberts supported **pasteurized milk** being delivered by dairies in glass bottles instead of metal pails. He also initiated universal **smallpox vaccinations**, as well as a medical checkup for every New Brunswick school child. The first **radium cancer treatment** in

New Brunswick was also his doing since he introduced radium therapy to Saint John.

Many of Robert's public health initiatives, while commonplace today, were innovations in preventive medicine that were highly controversial during the 1920s, especially the pasteurized versus raw milk controversy. The provincial milk producers fought Roberts over the pasteurization issue, contributing to his defeat in the 1925 provincial election. Although turned down at the polls, his legislation remained unchanged and William Roberts is today considered one of the pioneers of Canada's public health system.

Baby Safe

Doctor Beverly Brodie of Charlottetown and two friends created the Baby Safe product which they patented and produced for the retail market. The **Baby Safe device** consists of two rice bag weights connected to a pad which holds a sleeping baby and can be used to secure the baby on any flat surface. The device ensures a safe and comfortable sleep for infants by allowing a baby to sleep on its side without rolling over. The Prince Edward Island surgeon saw a need for such a product after her own daughter was born.

Politics

"Very few of us in this country share the same past, but all of us can share the same future." — Romeo LeBlanc upon becoming the first Acadian Governor General of Canada.

First Representative Government

After nearly three years of debate, the British Lords of Trade instructed Governor Lawrence to call an Assembly and the first **Representative Parliament** in what is now Canada, was assembled on October 2, 1758, in Halifax. The elected representatives formed a Legislative Assembly for Nova Scotia and first met under the auspices of a reluctant Governor Lawrence, who saw little advantage in sharing political power with an elected assembly.

Halifax merchant Robert Sanderson was appointed Speaker of the Assembly and David Lloyd became Clerk. Of the twenty-two Nova Scotians elected from across the colony, four were from Halifax and two from Lunenburg with a total of nineteen representatives attending Canada's first Parliament. Due to the religious and political prejudices of the day, voters had to be British, own freeheld property and could not be Catholic. Acadians, Blacks and Mi'kmaq were excluded yet the "foreign Protestants" of the Lunenburg area were quickly given citizenship and encouraged to vote.

Prince Edward Island was granted an elected assembly in 1773 and New Brunswick in 1784. While the colonial governor remained the single most powerful force in government matters, the 1758 assembly was the initial step toward responsible government, democracy, and nationhood. To commemorate the historic event, Sir Sandford Fleming and the Canadian Club of Halifax erected the Halifax Memorial Tower at Dingle Park on the Northwest Arm. In Province House, a memorial tablet erected in 1908 commemorated the 150th anniversary of the elected assembly and listed all attending members.

First Provincial Counties

In 1759, Nova Scotia became the first province in British North America to divide itself into **counties**. The first five counties were Annapolis, Kings, Cumberland, Lunenburg, and Halifax. Townships were also established that year, including Horton, Cornwallis, Cumberland, Lunenburg and Annapolis.

Canada's First Incorporated City

In 1783 thousands of United Empire Loyalists arrived at the mouth of the Saint John River and the following year New Brunswick became a colony separate from Nova Scotia with General Thomas Carleton as governor. Parrtown was renamed Saint John and received its Royal Charter from Governor Carleton in May 18, 1785, becoming the only **incorporated city** in British North America.

Designated the Loyalist City, Saint John had been mainly wilderness prior to 1783 and the rapid growth of wharves and trade throughout the harbour had resulted in the need for regulations and police enforcement. While provincial legislatures usually sponsor the establishment of municipalities, Saint John became unique in Canada in that the order of precedence was reversed. The city's charter antedated New Brunswick's initial legislative session. Using New York City's charter as a model, Carleton employed the former Boston lawyer, Ward Chipman, to produce Saint John's Charter, establishing a city corporation to enact by-laws and rules of trade over local matters. Entitled the Charter of the City of Saint John, it was printed by the local *Royal Gazette* publishers, William Lewis and John Ryan.

Gabriel Ludlow, who had commanded loyal forces against the American rebels on Long Island, was appointed the city's first mayor. As the architect of the city's charter, Loyalist Ward Chipman became city clerk and also served as the new province's solicitor general. While the mayor and city clerk were both appointed by Carleton, six aldermen were elected to the civil council by freemen of the city. Unfortunately the Black Loyalists who had arrived at Saint John as freemen were excluded from voting, since the original charter defined eligible freemen as "The American and European white inhabitants." Governor Carleton also disallowed Blacks from voting for the provincial Legislative Assembly. This restriction remained in place until at least 1840.

New Brunswick's first **Provincial Legislature** opened at the Mallard House in Saint John in 1786 but two years later, the provincial capital moved from Saint John to Fredericton. Yet Canada's first city managed to maintain its prominence within New Brunswick and by the mid-nineteenth century became the largest population and commercial centre in Atlantic Canada.

Political Riot

The first **political riot** in Canada occurred at the Mallard House in Saint John during the first provincial election in 1785. Election writs for the new province of New Brunswick were issued by Thomas Carleton for November 1785, with voting eligibility granted to all adult white males with three months residency. Government candidates for the six Saint John area seats were bitterly opposed by a large faction of disaffected men, who had received few privileges, especially in regard to land grants, from the New England-dominated Loyalist leaders. Headed by Elias Hardy, the discontented faction insisted on an elected assembly of freemen, who would be able to oppose privilege for the good of the majority.

When Sheriff William Oliver moved the poll from Hardy's headquarters at McPherson's Tavern in the Lower Cove to the government's headquarters at the Mallard House, Hardy's freemen attacked, breaking windows and doors and creating chaos. Troops from Fort Howe were called in to protect the Upper Cove area around King Street. The rebel leaders were arrested, fined and imprisoned, although Hardy managed to remain at large and later even became a member of the Legislature for Northumberland. The Lower Cove rebels won the majority of seats in the Saint John area but Governor Carleton insisted on a scrutiny and Sheriff Oliver reversed the results, declaring the government ticket, headed by Attorney General Jonathan Bliss, and Solicitor General Ward Chipman, as the winner.

Voting throughout the rest of the province went in favour of the government party, including Westmorland County where the sheriff disallowed the Acadian vote. In Saint John, despite wide discontent, the Upper

Cove party, composed of the ruling elite, remained dominant in the city's political life for some time.

Oldest Legislature Building

Province House in downtown Halifax is the **oldest Canadian legislature building** in use today. Designed by John Merrick and built with sandstone by architect Richard Scott, Canada's oldest seat of government was opened in 1819 after eight years of construction. Besides Joseph Howe's 1835 impassioned speech for freedom of the press, the House also witnessed Howe's fight for responsible government, the Confederation debates, and many other important political events.

Province House is often described as an almost perfect example of nineteenth-century Georgian architecture, "a gem of Georgian architecture" wrote Charles Dickens while visiting it in 1842. Province House features the magnificent Red Chamber, the Legislative Library, once the province's Supreme Court, as well as the Legislative Assembly, and the famous statute of Joseph Howe in the south courtyard. Although renovated with a new visitors gallery in 1866, the Assembly Chamber is still perhaps the smallest in the country, leading the touring Dickens to note that "it was like looking at Westminster through the wrong end of a telescope."

Prior to the age of air travel, royalty and new governors general would sail to Halifax from England and often were invested to office at Province House before travelling to Ottawa. For over 175 years, Province House has been the elegant seat of government in Nova Scotia, home to the first government in the British Empire to be responsible directly to its citizens.

Early Responsible Government

While representative government meant that some voters had a voice in government affairs, the British governor still retained full political control in colonial British North America. The establishment of **responsible government** in Canada occurred in Nova Scotia over an eight year period of political agitation. Finally on February 2, 1848 at Province House in Halifax, the first executive governing council was formed, chosen exclusively from the elected majority party.

Province House, Canada's oldest Legislature building, was built by workmen from Halifax's Royal Dockyards. (L.B. Jenson)

The Reform Party under Joe Howe had finally won a majority in the Legislative Assembly and was asked to form a government. Howe had begun the struggle eight years earlier by attacking the old unelected Executive Council in a speech that ended with: "The Executive Council as presently constituted does not enjoy the confidence of the Commons."

This new cabinet form of government was comprised exclusively of elected members of the majority party and remained under the leadership of the premier. The governing council became the supreme political authority of the province while the lieutenant governor, as a representative of the Crown, retained formal authority in Nova Scotia. Today's provincial structure of government is essentially similar with an elected leader, cabinet, and party, wielding political control.

Sir John Harvey had become lieutenant governor of Nova Scotia in 1846 and, as the supreme representative of the Crown in Nova Scotia, presided over the creation of responsible government in Canada by surrendering many of his colonial powers. With J.B. Uniacke as Premier and Attorney General, and Joseph Howe as Provincial Secretary and public spokesman, an Executive Council, composed of elected representatives of the Reform Party, was chosen and Nova Scotia became a self-governing province under the constitutional monarchy of the British Empire.

Upper Canada also was able to install this form of government, making it fully operational by the end of 1848. Prince Edward Island received responsible government in 1851 and New Brunswick in 1854. A memorial tablet in Province House, installed in 1948 by the Historic Sites and Monuments Board of Canada, commemorates the hundredth anniversary of Responsible Government in Canada.

Confederation

The first official conference leading to **Canadian Confederation** was the Charlottetown Conference, held on Prince Edward Island in September 1864. Initially a Maritime conference had been considered to discuss Maritime union. But a proposal from the United Upper and Lower Canadas, the Province of Canada, to discuss a possible political union of all British North America became the focus of the September conference.

Due to Britain's desire for a full confederation, as well as the external threat of the American Civil War, Maritime union was overshadowed as the notion of a United British North America was proposed by the six Canadian delegates. Maritimers were divided on the issue of a federal union. Many of the new railway communities backed confederation, while the older, ship-building seaports were uncertain of the economic advantages of linking with centres far inland.

At Charlottetown, the broad outlines of a confederation were sketched with support from Premier Charles Tupper of Nova Scotia and New Bruns-wick's Leonard Tilley. The delegates agreed to meet the following month and the Quebec Conference sealed the confederation agreement with Nova

Scotia, New Brunswick, Ontario and Quebec entering into full political union. Prince Edward Island declined union but entered Confederation on July 1, 1873.

To commemorate the historic Charlottetown meeting, the Confederation Centre of the Arts was constructed in Charlottetown in 1964 with financial contributions from all ten provinces. The centre's art gallery collection includes a significant portion of the Canadian works of Robert Harris, whose famous painting, *The Fathers of Confederation*, perished in the 1916 Parliament Buildings fire. A copy of the work hangs on a wall of the Confederation Chamber at Province House in Charlottetown, where the delegates first gathered in 1864.

Municipal Planning Act

Saint John passed the first **Town Planning Act** in Canada in 1912. Reaction from reformist citizens organizations to development efforts to construct a drydock on Courtney Bay, as well as the continued spread of slum housing, caused city council to enact an urban planning scheme. Surrounded on three sides by water, the city had been quickly rebuilt after the Great Fire of 1877 and with its patchwork pattern of streets, hewn out of rock, Saint John was judged to be overcrowded.

The act established zoning rules and regulations for orderly growth and urban renewal in Saint John, two years prior to the 1914 National Commission of Conservation's first International City Planning Conference in Toronto. The conference established the need for city planning throughout Canada and Saint John introduced a Town Planning Commission the same year. By the 1920s most cities in Canada had begun to implement some sort of zoning and development plans.

British Prime Minister

The first and only **Prime Minister of Britain** to have been born outside the British Isles was Andrew Bonar Law, who was born in New Brunswick in 1858. At age twelve, Law immigrated to Scotland. He later became wartime Chancellor of the Exchequer and in 1922, British Prime Minister. A close friend of Lord Beaverbrook, Law died in London in 1923. Today a cairn commemorates his birthplace at Rexton and his boyhood home along the

Richibucto River has become the nine hectare (22 acre) Bonar Law Historic Site.

Canada's Only Bilingual Province

New Brunswick became Canada's first official **Bilingual Province** in 1968 when New Brunswick's only elected Acadian premier, Louis Robichaud, passed the Official Languages Act, extending the French language throughout provincial government services and giving equal status to both languages. Robichaud had already introduced wide-reaching social reforms throughout New Brunswick with his Equal Opportunity program, established Université de Moncton, and increased the use of the French language throughout the province. His successor, Richard Hatfield, continued Robichaud's commitment to bilingualism and extended New Brunswickers' right to choice of language. Today, the province is still Canada's only official Bilingual Province.

Other Acadian leaders, especially Pierre Amand Landry, the first Acadian appointed to New Brunswick's **Supreme Court** in 1883, and New Brunswick's first **Acadian Premier**, Peter J. Veniot, made important contributions to establishing Acadian political presence in New Brunswick. Yet more than anyone, Louis Robichaud was responsible for bringing full and equal political rights to New Brunswick's Acadians.

Female Premier

Catherine Callbeck of Prince Edward Island became the first **woman elected Premier** in Canadian history when on March 29, 1993, she led the Island Liberal Party to a smashing victory, winning thirty-one of the thirty-two provincial seats. A resident of Central Bedeque, Callbeck was born in 1939 and graduated from Mount Allison and Dalhousie Universities. Before entering politics, Callbeck worked in her family's business, Callbeck's Ltd.

Acadian Governor General

On February 8, 1995, New Brunswick senator and former federal ministry of fisheries, Romeo LeBlanc, became Canada's first **Acadian Governor General**. In addressing the Senate Chamber, LeBlanc argued for national unity. As the Queen's representative in Canada, the former teacher, journalist, and folksy Liberal politician spoke passionately of his vision of a united Canada where ethnic differences are overcome as all Canadians contribute toward nation-building.

Education

"Mrs Bell had taken this method in her arms as a mother would take a child." — Marie Montessori during her visit to North America, thanking Mabel Bell for pioneering the Montessori teaching method in Canada and the US.

First Schools

Formal **schooling** in Canada began with the opening of a seminary in 1632 at Port Royal. The pioneering schoolmasters, members of the Capuchin Order of Missionaries from France, came to Acadia with Governor Isaac de Razilly. With Cardinal Richelieu as their patron, the Capuchin's mission was to convert the Mi'kmaq to Christianity, but in 1641 the seminary also admitted French children, including girls. By 1652, the school had prospered with two teachers and a headmistress, Madam de Brice D'Auxerre.

That same year, a French rogue trader named La Borgne seized Port Royal and the seminary was temporarily closed when the religious order was expelled. The school later reopened only to close permanently in 1654 when an English colonial force attacked Port Royal, burning the seminary.

The first **English school** in Canada also started near Port Royal and, like the earlier French school, was a religious institution. At nearby Annapolis Royal, the historic settlement served as the seat of English colonial government in Acadia between 1710 and 1749. In 1727 Richard Watts arrived in Annapolis Royal to become the first ordained clergyman of the Church of England to take up residency in Nova Scotia. Watts had two purposes at Annapolis: to serve as a chaplain for the garrison and establish a school for the religious instruction of the young, especially the poor.

The following Easter, using prayer books and tracts provided by the British Society for the Propagation of the Gospel in Foreign Parts, Watts began to hold classes. Watts was initially paid a yearly fee of £10 for his educational duties. The fee doubled in 1731 as the school expanded. After Watts left Nova Scotia for New England in 1738 the school was discontinued.

The early consolidated schools in the Maritimes were established in all provinces during the early 1900s, a result of Prince Edward Island millionaire tobacco tycoon Sir William Macdonald's offer to pay most costs for three years. The Tobacco King was convinced consolidated schools would provide better educational results for rural areas and paid all construction and equipment costs.

Macdonald even covered teacher salaries and a great deal of the transportation costs of operating horse-drawn vans and sleighs in order to bring the children back and forth to school. The first **consolidated school** in Canada, the Macdonald School, opened in 1903 at Middleton, Nova Scotia, and today is home to the Annapolis Valley Macdonald Museum. Consolidated schools were also opened in New Brunswick at Rexton, and on Prince Edward Island at Hillsboro, each replacing six or seven one-room schools. After the subsidy period ended, over half of the rural districts opted out due to higher costs as well as student preference for the old, familiar one-room schools.

Free Education for the Blind

Charles Frederick Fraser was born at Windsor in 1850 and became blind at age seven. Sent to the Perkins Institute in Boston, Fraser graduated at age twenty-two and immediately became principal of the Nova Scotia School for the Blind in Halifax. For nearly ten years, he fought stubbornly for improvements to the struggling educational institution and in 1882 convinced the Nova Scotia Legislature to enact a bill granting free education to blind residents of Nova Scotia.

As the first province or state to grant **free education to the blind**, Nova Scotia and Fraser's School for the Blind became innovators in blind education. Fraser's efforts led to the establishment of a **free lending library** for Braille books and in 1898, as a result of his persistent lobbying, the Canadian postal system granted **free postage** within Canada for Braille books.

Frederick Fraser worked incessantly for fifty years to improve conditions for blind people and made the Halifax School for the Blind one of the best in North America. Fraser was knighted for his efforts in 1915 and in 1939 his biography, *The Blind Knight of Nova Scotia*, appeared.

Montessori School

Mrs. Mabel Bell, wife of Alexander Graham Bell, established in 1912 the first **Montessori school** in Canada and the second in North America at her summer home, Beinn Bhreagh, outside of Baddeck. The Italian educator, Marie Montessori, had developed a system of education based on individual guidance and expression, rather than strict control. Mabel Bell, after visiting the first Montessori school on the American continent in upstate New York, encouraged a Montessori educator, Roberta Fletcher, to travel to Baddeck to instruct her grandchildren.

Bell's daughter Daisy Fairchild, also interested in progressive education, helped organize the classes. The initial class was held in the upper storey of the Beinn Bhreagh warehouse and comprised eight children, mainly pre-school in age, including children of the workers at the estate. The guiding educational principle was to avoid force feeding the children by carefully laying out selected materials and letting their natural curiosity take over.

Bell also sponsored another Montessori school that same autumn in the annex of her own home in Washington, DC. The following spring, a permanent school opened and Bell formed the Montessori Educational Association in order to promote the new principles of education. The association also began publishing an educational magazine and the following winter Madame Montessori began a lecture tour throughout North America, warmly praising Mrs. Bell's pioneering efforts.

Home and School Association

Besides her role as the wife of one of the most famous inventors in the world, Mabel Bell was herself an innovator and open to new ideas, especially in educational matters. Besides her involvement with Montessori education, Mabel Bell in 1895 organized the first **Home and School Association** in Canada at Baddeck.

Born to wealthy parents in 1857, Mabel Hubbard became deaf at age five from scarlet fever. At nineteen, she married her teacher and telephone inventor, Alexander Graham Bell. While living in Washington, DC, Mrs. Bell

Educational pioneer Mabel Bell and family, including Alexander Graham, at Baddeck, Nova Scotia during their first visit in 1885. (Library of Congress)

had taken part in a women's group called the Washington Club that met regularly to discuss ideas of mutual interest, including political, artistic and literary issues. Back in Baddeck, Bell helped organize a similar women's group, initially called the Young Ladies Club of Baddeck and then the Alexander Graham Bell Club.

After Alexander Bell addressed the group about efforts by parents to form associations in the American schools for the deaf, a number of parents involved in the Baddeck Academy established a similar association. This first Canadian Home and School Association developed a number of parent-teacher programs, emphasizing the welfare of youth and encouraging better family life. The financially well-off Mabel Bell supported their work, which led to a number of community improvement projects, including establishment of Baddeck's first public library.

Boy Scouts

In 1908 at Port Morien, Cape Breton, William Glover started the first **Boy Scout troop** in Canada. The troop began by meeting at Glover's home and then at the local Blockhouse school. Initially, the Scout troop consisted of eleven boys. Glover had come from England to work in the Cape Breton coal industry and agreed with the first Scout, Lord Baden Powell that "Scouting is mainly a great adventure played out of doors." Without an established agenda, Glover encouraged the boys to hike and engage in other outdoor activities.

St Ann's Gaelic College

The first **Gaelic college** in North America opened at St. Ann's, Cape Breton, on July 26, 1939. Established to foster and develop the Gaelic language, the Gaelic College of Arts and Crafts also acquired a mandate to promote and cultivate the traditional Celtic art forms, including music and dance. The founder and first director of the college was Rev. A.W.R. MacKenzie, a native of the Isle of Skye in Scotland. Ironically, MacKenzie did not speak Gaelic, yet many of the instructors did, including Jonathan G. MacKinnon, the founder of the first Gaelic newspaper in North America, MacTalla. A Gaelic Mod is organized each summer at St. Ann's as a traditional Cape Breton Scottish festival.

Universities of the Maritimes

In 1875, Grace Annie Lockhart received her Bachelor's degree in Science and English Literature from Mount Allison University, the first **woman graduate** from any degree-granting college in the British Empire. Seven years later, Mount Allison's Harriet Stewart became the first woman in Canada to receive a **Bachelor of Arts degree**. Chartered in 1858 at Sackville, Mount Allison included an educational faculty for women and featured a liberal and fine arts undergraduate program.

One of the first universities in Canada to establish a Fine Arts program as well as to award Fine Arts degrees, Mount Allison is home to the **oldest university art gallery** in Canada, the Owens Art Gallery. Saint John shipbuilder John Owens had established the art collection as part of the port city's art school and his estate agreed to its move to Sackville in 1895. Saint John artist John Hammond also arrived to head the Fine Arts Department and in 1941, Mount Allison became the first Canadian university to offer a **Bachelor of Fine Arts**.

Mount Saint Vincent University in Halifax began in 1873 as a women's Catholic academy and was given degree-granting status in 1925, the first **independent college for women** in the British Commonwealth.

The first **Catholic co-educational institution** of higher learning in North America was St. Francis Xavier University of Antigonish. Founded in 1853 in Arichat, Cape Breton, St. Francis moved to Antigonish two years later and first became co-educational in 1894, after affiliating with Mount St. Bernard College. Degrees were first awarded to four women in 1897.

St. Francis Xavier University recognized the demands of students in the 1960s to have a say in university affairs by appointing in 1968 an undergraduate to the **University's Board of Governors**. Mike McIntosh became the first undergraduate student in Canada to sit on a university's governing board.

Acadia University was established in 1839 by the Baptist Education Society of Nova Scotia. With little colonial financial support for its programs, which were seen as inspired by Baptist theology, Acadia in 1859 founded the first **university alumni organization** in Canada. Annual membership fees were established at twenty shillings. In 1915, John Daniel Logan started one of the first university courses in Canada devoted exclusively to **Canadian**

literature. Logan returned to Acadia after World War I as a full-time professor, specializing in Canadian literature.

Canada's **oldest chartered university**, University of King's College, was established in 1789 by the Anglican Church under the direction of Bishop Inglis, at Windsor, Nova Scotia. The Bishop's son, John Inglis, became the first student to enroll at King's, considered one of the first residential boys school in Canada. The first chartered university in the Commonwealth, King's received degree-granting status in 1802 but a major fire in 1920 forced its move to Halifax and alignment with Dalhousie University. Today, except for its journalism program, most degrees are awarded in conjunction with Dalhousie University.

Dalhousie University was founded by Lieutenant Governor George Ramsay on the Grand Parade in Halifax and modelled after the educational philosophy of Edinburgh University. Under its first president, Pictou educator Thomas McCulloch, Dalhousie achieved degree-granting status in 1841 and its law school, established in 1883 by Robert Sedgewick, became the first in the British Empire to teach **common law**.

In 1890, Sedgewick, along with Judge Burbridge, drafted the Canadian Criminal Code. Well known for its ocean science, law, and medical research, as well as its graduate studies, Dalhousie moved in 1887 from the downtown to its present southwest Halifax location.

Saint Mary's University was founded in Halifax in 1841 by Rev. Edmund Burke, the first **English Catholic institution** of higher learning in Canada, while the first **English-speaking Catholic seminary**, St Margaret's, was also established in Halifax in 1819. In 1970, Saint Mary's became a lay university with an independent board of governors and is today well known for its undergraduate programs.

The Nova Scotia College of Art and Design is unique in Canada in that it is the only university specializing in the **visual arts**. Now offering both undergraduate and graduate degrees, NSCAD began in 1887 as Halifax's Victoria School of Art and Design largely through local efforts, including assistance from the acclaimed Anna Leonowens, the heroine of Rodgers and Hammerstein's *The King and I*.

Canada's **oldest provincial university**, the University of New Brunswick, was established as a Provincial Academy in 1785 at Fredericton. Like Nova Scotia's King's College, New Brunswick's university was modelled after the Loyalist institution, King's College in New York, now Columbia University, and received its educational charter in 1800 and its royal charter as King's College in 1828. The Old Arts Building (1825-29) is Canada's **oldest university building** still in use today. Built entirely in stone by J.F. Woolford, the following inscription is carved into the centre stone on the roof of the portico: A.D. 1829 John Murray, Master Stone Cutter.

The first formal **civil engineering course** in Canada was established in 1854 at the Fredericton University. William Brydone Jack, with encouragement from New Brunswick's Lieutenant Governor Sir Edmund Head, convinced the New Brunswick Legislature to finance an engineering course to provide students with practical surveying expertise. The first **engineering student** to graduate was Henry Ketchum.

During the mid-1900s, Canada was in critical need of engineers to tap the nation's huge resource wealth, as well as to build railways, roads and cities for the emerging country. William Brydone Jack was especially interested in the new, applied sciences. As president of the university for over twenty years, he also established the first **standards laboratory** in Canada for surveying instruments and was largely responsible for UNB's emergence during the late 1800s as an important Canadian centre of learning in the practical sciences.

William Brydone Jack's most outstanding achievement was in the field of astronomy. In 1851 he established an astronomical observatory on the UNB campus, now called the Brydone Jack Observatory. Despite an earlier observatory at Louisbourg, an official plaque identifies the building as the first astronomical observatory in Canada. It is certain, however, that Brydone Jack's building is the **oldest observatory still in existence** in Canada. Brydone also is credited as giving the first public lectures on astronomy in Canada

While chemistry was first taught in Canada in Quebec, it seems that the first full university course in **chemistry** was taught by James Robb at the University of New Brunswick in 1837. Robb had been appointed professor of chemistry and natural science, which then included biology as well as botany.

Université de Moncton's Law School is the only law school in Canada teaching **civil law** in the French language. The university was established in

1963 at Moncton by the amalgamation of three smaller Acadian educational institutions in New Brunswick.

Adult Education Pioneers

The founder of **adult education** in Canada was Rev. Alfred Fitzpatrick, a Pictou County Presbyterian minister who became a missionary in isolated mining, logging and railway camps. Realizing the need for basic adult education, Fitzpatrick organized **Frontier College** in 1899 where young university students would volunteer to work in northern work camps and teach workers basic reading, writing and math skills. Educated at Pictou Academy and Queens University, Fitzpatrick was one of the first to recognize the enormous social problem of illiteracy. Incorporated by Parliament in 1922, Frontier College received the UNESCO award for achievement in adult literacy in 1977.

Other early pioneers in adult education were the two priests from Margaree, Cape Breton — Jimmy Tompkins and Moses Coady. Together they founded the Antigonish Movement through the Extension Department of St. Francis Xavier University at Antigonish during the 1920s. The concept of evening classes for the farmers and fishermen of Nova Scotia in order to develop their skills and encourage co-operatives and community self-reliance was quite revolutionary and quickly spread to other parts of Canada.

Sport

"The Saint John men were thoroughly on their mettle and the gap was widening, when Renforth turned his head and giving a look at his opponent's boat, dropped his oar, threw up an arm and would have fallen overboard had he not been caught by Kelly, who supported him, while Percy and Chambers rowed the shell ashore." — Saint John *Telegraph-Journal*'s account of the 1871 Paris–Tyne race where famous British oarsman Renforth collapsed of heart failure.

Skating and the New Skates

The earliest record of **skating** in North America arises in De Monts' expedition at St. Croix Island, during the first winter, 1604. Besides hunting and downing rabbits in cold weather, the young men went "skating on the ponds," according to Port Royal historian Marc Lescarbot. The winter was bitterly cold at the temporary island settlement in the St. Croix River, which today makes up the border between New Brunswick and Maine.

John Forbes of the Starr Manufacturing Company in Dartmouth invented the world's first all **steel spring skate** in 1866. The new high quality metal skate allowed for the development of hockey and figure skating by eliminating the brittle, wooden skate. While a permanently installed skate blade on a boot was not introduced until the 1920s, the Acme Forbes skate did revolutionize skating, creating worldwide demand for this new skate, including an order from the King of Spain.

The **Long Reacher skate** came into being through the efforts of James Whelphey in 1875 at Long Reach, on New Brunswick's Saint John River. This long skate was ideally suited to skating over the clear ice of lakes and large rivers of the Lower Saint John River Valley. Whelphey's skates were similar to today's racing skates except that they were fastened to boots by a pair of straps at the heel and toe, rather than being rivetted to skating boots. The skate itself consisted of a blade inserted into a wooden platform.

Exported worldwide in the late 1800s, the long skate increased the popularity of marathon skating events, often covering distances of eighty kilometres (50 miles) or more. As a result of this new skate, a popular New Brunswick winter challenge developed that involved skating from Saint John to Fredericton and return. A Whelphey skate factory was established at Jones Creek near Saint John, turning out the famous Long Reachers on which several New Brunswick skaters won world speed-skating championships. Saint John became the marathon skate capital as Whepley set a world record skating 187 kilometres (117 miles) in ten hours.

The first known organized **indoor speed skating competition** in Canada took to the ice in 1883 at Saint John's Victoria Skating Rink on City Road. Built in 1865, the indoor rink supported a grand dome resting on a huge, circular six metre (20 feet) high wall. Gas jets illuminated this architectural delight and included a spiral staircase leading to two cascaded, circular galleries. Masquerade and dress carnival skating were popular events at the Vic.

Sailing Club and The First Regatta

The Royal Nova Scotia Yacht Squadron, now situated on the Northwest Arm, Halifax, is the **oldest continuously operating yacht club** in Canada and possibly North America. Established in 1837 as the Halifax Yacht Club, seven years before the New York Yacht Club was formed, its first president was the Hon. T. N. Jeffery, while the club's first treasurer was the wealthy Halifax merchant, Enos Collins.

The Nordbeck Cup, made by noted Nova Scotian silversmith, Peter Nordbeck, was awarded to the winner of the club's first regatta. The club was renamed the Royal Halifax Yacht Club in 1861 after receiving royal patronage during the Prince of Wales' 1860 visit. Besides consenting to be the club's patron, the Prince donated the Prince of Wales Challenge Cup on the condition that it be raced for on the first of August each year. In 1880, the club became the Royal Nova Scotia Yacht Club.

The first **sailing regatta** in Canada is reported to have also taken place in Halifax on July 17, 1826, as part of a program arranged for the visit of

Lord Dalhousie. Primarily organized by the Royal Navy, Rear Admiral Willoughby Lake won first class with his sloop, the *Emily*. Besides naval races, a special fisherman class race was established to encourage the large number of civilian vessels to complete. However, the most popular race occurred on the final day when Mi'kmaq in four canoes raced from the Halifax waterfront to George's Island and back.

Antigonish Highland Games

The earliest **Highland Games** in Canada was staged by the Caledonian Club of Prince Edward Island in 1838, but the oldest continuing Highland Games in North America began in 1863 at Antigonish. The games were organized by the Antigonish Highland Society, which had formed two years earlier to promote the Scottish-Gaelic culture throughout eastern Nova Scotia. The *Antigonish Casket* reported the society's aim was to keep up "the noble spirit and memory of Old Scotia." The Highland Games, emphasizing Scottish events including tossing the caber, heavy hammer throwing, highland fling, as well as Scottish pageantry embodied in music and dance.

The first meet included prizes for the seven kilogram (16 pounds) heavy hammer event, the eleven kilogram (24 pounds) heavy stone, throwing the six metre (20 feet) caber, running, as well as playing the bag pipes and dancing the Highland fling. Novelty events included the wheelbarrow and sack races, and society members were encouraged to purchase the competitors registration tickets at twenty-five cents each. Less than fifteen years later, the games had grown considerably and a gold medal was awarded to the winner of the hammer throw, who was then crowned the Nova Scotian champion. Later fiddling, bagpiping, Gaelic dancing, singing and readings were added as the Highland Games became a major tourist attraction and cultural event for eastern Nova Scotia.

With a few wartime exceptions, the annual games have endured in Antigonish and are always held the second weekend of July. Highland games are now staged throughout North America and Scotland, but the Antigonish Highland Games are considered a unique symbol of Nova Scotia's Scottish heritage.

Hockey, Halifax, and James Creighton

While Canada is indeed the country that originated the game of ice hockey, where the first game was played is difficult to determine. The game developed out of the early stick and ball games called hurley, shinny, or bandy that were played on frozen ponds and lakes throughout Canada. Halifax, Saint John, Windsor, Nova Scotia, Montreal, Quebec City and Kingston, Ontario, all claim to be the cradle of ice hockey.

As early as 1805, the Nova Scotia *Royal Gazette* reported a form of cricket was being played on ice on the Northwest Arm at Halifax and in the 1820s, Mi'kmaq were seen playing their game of hurley on the Dartmouth lakes as well as on Saint John's Lily Lake. Thomas Haliburton reported seeing students from Windsor's King's College playing similar ice games on nearby Long Pond. British troops garrisoned at Halifax, the Royal Canadian Rifles, reportedly played hockey in 1855 and one game played that same year by British troops in Kingston, involved fifty men per team.

Based on games of shinny played in the 1860s, Kingston has been accepted by the Hockey Hall of Fame as hockey's birthplace. We do know, however, that the first organized ice hockey recognized as today's game was played in 1875 at the indoor Victoria Ice Rink in Montreal. The historic game is often cited as Canada's first real game of hockey and if so, James Creighton of Halifax can be considered the **Father of Hockey** since he is reported to have proposed the game and the "Halifax Rules" for playing it. Creighton has never received the credit due such a hockey pioneer who more than anyone, established hockey's first rules by importing the Halifax game to Montreal. As Creighton's teammate and Montreal merchant, Henry Joseph, told the *Montreal Gazette* in 1936, "J.G.A. Creighton was responsible for the start of hockey here."

James Creighton was born in Halifax in 1850 and attended the Halifax Grammar School and Dalhousie University, before moving to Montreal in 1872 to work as a railway construction engineer. After seeing an attempt to play lacrosse on ice fail, he proposed a stick and ball game to Henry Joseph, based on the ice games he had seen played on the Northwest Arm and the Dartmouth lakes. Joseph reported that Creighton acquired sticks from Halifax and actually captained the winning team in its 2-1 victory over a team of McGill students.

The world famous Paris crew of Saint John at their training headquarters in Southampton, England with their business manager Sheriff Harding. From left to right behind their scull are Robert Fulton, Elijah Ross, Samuel Hutton, and George Price. (New Brunswick Museum, Saint John, NB)

The historic 1875 game was promoted in advance by the *Montreal Gazette* which reported that nine men were used per side. Instead of a rubber ball, a flat, circular piece of wood was reportedly used, the first confirmed reference to today's hockey puck, although a rubber puck was claimed to have been introduced in 1872 by Halifax goaltender William Gill. Creighton went on to a distinguished career as a journalist, scholar and lawyer, serving as law clerk to the Canadian Senate.

Regarding professional hockey, the Maritimes can claim the first **Black professional hockey player.** Fredericton native William Eldon "Willie" O'Ree played his first game as a Boston Bruins' forward in 1958 on January 18, against the Montreal Canadiens. Willie O'Ree played in the professional leagues, including the NHL for a number of years before retiring in the 1960s.

Paris Crew, a Rowing Legend

In 1867 the celebrated Paris Crew of Saint John became the first Canadian **four-oared rowing crew** to win a world championship. Robert Fulton, Elijah Ross, Samuel Hutton, and George Price, New Brunswick's entry in the World's Exposition international regatta at Paris, won two races despite a heavy, obsolete boat that was judged too wide for maximum rowing efficiency. Using an unconventional short, quick stroke, forty-one strokes per minute, the Paris Crew dominated foursome international rowing until they were defeated in 1870 by England's famous Tyne Crew led by the legendary James Renforth.

The rematch took place in August 1871, outside Saint John on the Kennebecasis River. It attracted thousands of spectators for the ten-kilometre (6 mile) event. Observers and the press from all over North America and Europe occupied every available viewing spot on both embankments, as they watched this championship sculling contest.

Hotly contesting the first kilometre (.6 mile), the English crew attempted to halt New Brunswick's half-a-length break, when their leader James Renforth collapsed apparently of heart failure, dying the next morning. The Paris Crew crossed the finish line the winner in just over thirty-nine minutes, not knowing the other boat's fate. The river village Chalet near Rothesay, was later renamed Renforth in honour of this champion British oarsman.

Canada's First Baseball Player

The Canadian to first play **major league baseball** was William Phillips of Saint John. Born in 1857, he played for the Cleveland Indians beginning in 1879, manning first base throughout his ten-year career in the big leagues. Phillips hit .271 his first year as Cleveland finished a disappointing sixth in the eight-team National League, compiling a win-loss record of 27–55.

In 1885, Phillips moved to the American Association and played for Brooklyn, where he had his best year hitting .302, while continuing to play first base. He finished his career with Kansas City of the AA league in 1888 with a major league hitting average of .266. He died at the age of forty-three while living in Chicago.

League of her Own

Edna Lockhart Duncanson was born in the Annapolis Valley at Avonport and in 1935 signed with the New York Bloomergirls to became the first **Canadian female professional baseball player**. At seveteen, she happened to be visiting her sister in New York and began playing catch with a friend.

Her baseball talents were obvious to everyone and she began playing with the Bloomergirls the next day. Travelling at night in two open cars, the Depression era meant the girls often stayed in old hotels and ate cheaply. But their manager enforced strict rules on the players with many do's and don'ts, including no cigarettes or beer. In her late seventies, Edna Duncanson now lives near her birthplace in the Gaspereau Valley.

Early Basketball

Basketball was invented by Canadian physical education instructor James Naismith at Springfield, Massachusetts, in the fall of 1891. Naismith established thirteen rules for the indoor game that was first played with a soccer ball and peach baskets nailed to the gymnasium balcony. Initially, it was necessary for players to use a ladder in order to get up and retrieve the basketball. Basketball was instantly successful and became part of the YMCA's indoor physical education program.

The new game of basketball was first **played in Canada** in 1892 at St. Stephen, by Nova Scotian Lyman Archibald, one of the original students to play with Naismith at Springfield. Archibald was a member of Naismith's first school team at the Springfield YMCA Teacher Training School that included two other Maritime players. He graduated in the spring of 1892 and moved to the St. Stephen area to work as a YMCA instructor and brought his knowledge of basketball back to Canada, teaching the game during the fall of 1892. About the same time, another of Naismith's students, T.D. Patton, introduced the game in Montreal.

As an alternative to calisthenics and marching exercises, basketball immediately was popular as an indoor winter sport and rapidly began to flourish in Canadian towns and cities. Archibald eventually became General Secretary of the Canadian YMCA and developed a number of the physical education programs in the early 1900s.

A Boxing Pioneer

George Dixon of Halifax became a boxing legend by being the first to win **world boxing titles** in three divisions, featherweight, paperweight, and bantamweight. Fighting under the stage name of Little Chocolate, Dixon held the featherweight title for ten years and retired as the undefeated bantamweight champion. Born in 1870 at Africville on the Bedford Basin, Dixon began his career in Halifax at sixteen, weighing thirty-nine kilograms (87 pounds). He moved to Boston still an amateur fighter, achieving more in sport than almost any other Maritimer. Fully matured as a fighter, Dixon was unusually small at 1.6 metres (5 feet, 3 inches) and fifty-two kilograms (115 pounds), yet he was one of the most brilliant boxers of the 1890s. A boxing pioneer who invented **shadow boxing** and the **suspended punching bag**, Dixon reportedly had exceptional speed and defensive skills. In 1890, he went the distance in a gruelling twenty-two-round bout in Britain.

Ten years as champion left him complacent and in less than peak condition, yet he continued to fight until his health deteriorated after more than thirty title defences. He died at thirty-nine, penniless and in poor health. His exceptional career ended in a fifteen-round loss in 1906 to a virtual unknown, "Monk the Newsboy," at Providence, Rhode Island. George Dixon encountered racism throughout his career but managed to break through the colour barrier to become the first **Black man to win a world boxing title**. Dixon was also the first boxer to **win more than one boxing title** and to win under the Marquis of Queensberry rules. A recreation centre on Gottingen Street in Halifax commemorates this outstanding boxer.

Marathoner Johnny Miles

Cape Breton runner Johnny Miles travelled by train from his home in Sydney Mines, to Boston in 1926 to become the first Canadian to win the **Boston Marathon** on its new Olympic standard course of forty-two kilometres (26.2 miles). The classic marathon distance of 42.195 kilometres was established at the London Olympics of 1908 by Princess Mary so that she could conveniently start the race at the royal nursery. First organized in 1897, the Boston Marathon extended its race distance in 1924 to meet the international standard.

A number of Canadians including Nova Scotian Fred Cameron had previously won Boston on the shorter course, but Miles established a new course and world record of two hours twenty-five minutes in 1926, almost four minutes faster than record holder Clarence DeMar's time. Unknown to the Boston Marathon organizers, and untested at the distance, the twenty-year-old Cape Bretoner beat both Demar and the Olympic champion Albin

Stenroos of Finland. Unable to finish in 1927, Miles won again in 1929. Clarence DeMar, Boston's most famous marathoner,who won Boston a record seven times, described Johnny Miles' first Boston win as "phenomenal." One of the most talented Maritime athletes to compete internationally, Johnny Miles became a member of the Canadian Sports Hall of Fame in 1967. A marathon named in his honour is organized each spring in New Glasgow.

First Curling Brier

The winner of the initial **Canadian men's curling championship**, the Brier Tankard, was the Halifax Curling Club, skipped by Dalhousie professor Murray McNeill. Held at the Granite Club in Toronto in 1927, a total of eight rinks participated from across Canada. The other members of the victory team were also from the Halifax Curling Club, first started in 1824. The trophy and championship was sponsored by the W.D. Macdonald Tobacco Co. and the annual event led to a significant increase in the sport's popularity throughout Canada. The 1927 Brier was the only year clubs were allowed to bring their own stones to the national brier.

The Dartmouth Paddler

The first Canadian to win seven North American Championships in **paddling** as well as the first to win the Canadian Juvenile, Junior, and Senior Championship in succession, was Christopher Brian Hook of Dartmouth. Paddling competitively on the Dartmouth lakes at age eleven, Chris Hook was Canada's top juvenile hope for an international medal when at age seventeen, he contacted a rare polio virus. He recovered and slowly began to train again, representing one of Dartmouth's major clubs, the Banook Canoe Club. In 1965, Hook won the Canadian Junior Championship and in 1966, became the North American winner in both the Junior and Senior C-1 1,000. Again in 1967, Hook won the gold at the North American Championships in the C-1 1,000 and 10,000 events.

Training somewhat in isolation, with little direct coaching, Chris Hook became the best paddler in North America in the late 1960s. At age twenty-one, he won the Canadian Olympic trials and represented Canada at the Mexico City Olympics. As Canada's only medal hope in canoeing,

Hook made the finals in the 1,000 metre (3,280 feet) singles event but despite leading the race at 250 metres (820 feet), he performed poorly at high altitude, finishing well back of the eastern Europeans. He moved to Europe and trained under a Hungarian coach between 1969 and 1971, but placed a disappointing fourth in the 1971 world championships in Belgrade and retired the same year. A product of the pre-scientific paddling era in the region, Chris Hook was undoubtedly one of the most successful athletes to emerge from the Dartmouth lakes, a hotbed for canoeing in the Maritimes.

Religion

"The first time I baptized here was a little before Christmas, in the creek which ran through my lot. I preached to a great number on the occasion, who behaved very well. I now formed the church with us six, and administered the Lord's Supper in the Meeting-house before it was finished." — David George's recollection of the initial meeting of the first Black Baptist Church in Canada.

Membertou and the First Catholic Missionary

Jessé Fléché arrived at the small Port Royal colony in 1610 to become the earliest known **Roman Catholic missionary** to settle in Canada. Officials considered Fléché a secular priest since his commission had not been issued by a French priest but by the Papal Nuncio in Paris. Fléché undertook the first **native baptism** in New France when he baptized the local Mi'kmaq chief, Henri Membertou, as well as the chief's family.

Sagamos or Chief Membertou was already an old man at the time of the Port Royal settlement and had remembered the arrival of Jacques Cartier fifty years earlier. Membertou's entrepreneurial instinct was excellent as he immediately became the small colony's native partner, trading for furs and acting as the colony's agent in dealing with other native tribes.

Membertou guarded the Habitation for three years, while the French returned to France in a dispute over their monopoly. He was baptized on Saint John Baptist Day in 1610 and given the French name Henri after the late French king. Membertou soon contacted the white man's disease, dysentery, and died the next year after being treated by the first doctor in Acadia, Louis Hébert.

Jessé Fléché was nicknamed the "Patriarch" by the Mi'kmaq, but was not really successful in converting the native people to Catholicism. Unable to speak Mi'kmaq, he enlisted Charles De Beincourt to administer the catechism in the Mi'kmaq language. After one winter at Acadia, Fléché returned to France at the same time that the next Catholic missionaries arrived.

First Jesuits

The **Jesuits** arrived at Port Royal from France in June 1611. Fathers Pierre Biard and Enemond Massé sailed with Charles de Biencourt from Dieppe, complete with the blessing and financial support of the Queen of France. Founded in Paris in 1534 by a Spanish soldier, the Society of Jesus became a strict religious order, emphasizing obedience to the papacy and excellence in education.

Biard and Massé continued the missionary work of the secular priest, Jessé Fléché, attempting to convert the Indians to Christianity, but they quarrelled with the Port Royal authorities, especially Charles de Biencourt and his father. Pierre Biard was an especially determined missionary and lived with the Mi'kmaq, converting a number of them. For a short time, he established a Jesuit community near Mount Desert Island in Maine but was captured by English raiders and sent back to France. Father Massé returned to France too but later sailed to Quebec with Jean de Brebeuf to found the Huron Jesuit Mission.

Church of England

Following the capture of Fort Anne by British troops under Francis Nicholson in 1710, Rev. John Harrison held the first **Church of England service** in Canada on the old fort grounds at Annapolis Royal. Richard Watts was the first duly **ordained clergyman** of the British church to establish residency in Canada when he arrived at Annapolis Royal in 1727 and established the first English school.

St. Paul's Church

St. Paul's Church was constructed on Halifax's Grand Parade in 1750 and is considered the earliest **Protestant church** in Canada as well as the first public building erected in Halifax. Built with pine timbers and oak frames brought by ship from Boston, St. Paul's was modelled on James Gibbs' drawings of Marybone Chapel in London.

The first **service** was held in the church September 2, 1750, and the initial **Protestant orphanage** in Canada was started at St. Paul's four years later. An organ was obtained in 1765 from a captured Spanish ship and the first oratorio performed in a Canadian church occurred at St. Paul's in 1769. In 1783 the first **Sunday School** was also conducted there. The church has the distinction of having the only English **church register** in Canada maintained under the old Julian calendar.

Bishop Inglis conducted the first Church of England **ordination** there in 1788. Inglis himself the previous year had been consecrated the first **Anglican bishop** in the British Empire with a diocese that included all of the Atlantic Provinces, as well as Ontario and Quebec. Twenty burial vaults lie beneath the church containing prominent Nova Scotians, including Governor Charles Lawrence, who ordered the Expulsion of the Acadians in 1755.

First Baptist Church

The initial **Baptist congregation** in Canada was formed at Sackville, New Brunswick, in 1763 by settlers from Massachusetts under Rev. Nathan Mason and flourished for almost ten years. Called the General Six Principle Baptist Church because its theology was based on the six principles in Hebrews 6.2, the church emphasized free will and personal responsibility, similar to the later New Light and Free Baptist churches.

The earliest **Baptist ordination** in Canada was held at Wolfville in 1778 when Nicholas Pierson was ordained as pastor. Founded in 1765 by Ebenezer Moulton, who became the first **Baptist Minister** in Canada when he settled at Yarmouth in 1761, the Wolfville church was re-covenanted in 1788, solely as a Baptist church. Today the Wolfville United Baptist Church is recognized as having the **oldest continuing Baptist congregation** in Canada.

One of the most important religious figures in Canada and the founder of the **New Light** evangelical movement in the Maritimes was the charismatic preacher Henry Alline. Alline's theology was similar to the early Baptist, especially regarding its opposition to Calvinism, and today, the New Light movement is often considered an early Baptist sect.

Born in Newport, Rhode Island, Alline moved to the Annapolis Valley at twelve with his Planter family, farming land abandoned by the expelled Acadians. A religious experience in 1775 convinced Alline of the need to preach God's message of direct religious experience and personal faith. The New Light Movement, similar to the Great Awakening in New England, swept throughout the Maritimes with Alline the undisputed leader. His published hymns described in verse his spiritual journey and while his ministry only lasted seven years, Alline's influence among the Maritime Baptist movement remains substantial. He died of consumption in New England In 1703.

Black Baptist Missionary

The first **Black Baptist pastor** in Canada as well as the first **Baptist missionary** to Africa was Loyalist David George. Born in Virginia, the son of African slaves, George organized the first Black Baptist church in North America, the Silver Bluff Baptist Church in Sliver Bluff, Georgia. Arriving in Shelburne in 1783, George's impassioned preaching style attracted a congregation of about fifty blacks and whites to his services, considered the initial congregation of the second oldest Baptist church in Canada, the Shelburne Baptist church.

This Shelburne congregation was the beginning of the **Black Baptist church** in Canada and as the only Black organization at the time, the early Maritime Black Baptist movement quickly grew into a political voice for Blacks with Rev. David George one of its leaders. Racial hatred and anger by disbanded soldiers over Blacks accepting lower wages, led in 1784 to a mob of whites preventing a baptism at his service, forcing George from his chapel and the Shelburne area. Recalling the incident later for the *Baptist Register*, George had insisted on preaching despite persecution until "they came and beat me with sticks, and drove me into the swamp."

George continued his ministry and travelled throughout the Maritimes, establishing Baptist chapels for Blacks at Preston, Liverpool, and Horton, as well as undertaking the first baptisms in Saint John. Along with Richard Preston, David George can be considered one of the founders of the African Baptist Church of Nova Scotia. Discouraged with poor treatment and constant harassment, he joined Thomas Peters, Boston King, and almost

1,200 other Blacks on January 15, 1792, setting sail from Halifax in fifteen ships to Sierra Leone, quickly establishing a Baptist ministry at Freetown. Rev. David George spent his remaining days preaching the gospel in Sierra Leone. One of the few Black Loyalists to have left a published record, George travelled to London from Sierra Leone and dictated his memories to the editor of the *Baptist Annual Register*.

Oldest Nonconformist Church

The **oldest existing Nonconformist church** in Canada, the Old Meeting House, at Barrington, Nova Scotia, was built in 1765 by Cape Cod settlers. Constructed with heavy oak and pine, its exposed ceiling beams are braced for support with "ships knees," installed by the early shipbuilding carpenters. The Meeting House also served the community as a civic centre, especially for New England-style town meetings, and today is a museum that still holds occasional religious services, including one the third Sunday of every August.

An **evangelical service** was conducted in 1767 by Samuel Wood and during the 1780s, Rev. Henry Alline preached his New Light sermons at the historic meeting centre. Other congregations that held services there include the Methodists, Congregationalists, Presbyterians, Anglicans, Free Baptists, and Baptists. The old Barrington Meeting House is now operated as a provincial museum, while the grounds include a burial site where some of the first settlers are enshrined, including two early minsters, Rev. Thomas Crowell and Rev. Edward Reynolds.

Presbyterian Church

The first **Presbyterian ordination** in Canada was held in 1770 at Lunenburg, when Bruin Romkes Comingo was ordained a minister of the Dutch Calvinist Church. St. Andrew's Church, the first **Presbyterian church** in Canada, was built at Lunenburg in 1754 and rebuilt on the same site in 1828.

Little Dutch Church

The Little Dutch Church at Brunswick and Gerrish Streets, Halifax was erected in 1756 as a small log cottage, the first **Lutheran church** in Canada. The Lutheran congregation was made up of European or Foreign Protestants, mainly German, but also Swiss, Dutch and French who immigrated to Halifax from continental Europe during 1750. Most Lutherans were resettled in the Lunenburg area, but about twenty-five German families remained in north-end Halifax, transforming the small building, measuring twelve metres by six metres (40 by 20 feet), into a handsome but modest meeting house. The cottage also served as the tiny community's church and school. Also called the German Meeting House, the Little Dutch Church, while still standing, is no longer used for services.

St. George's Round Church was constructed nearby in 1800 in accommodate the growing north-end Halifax community and is considered the first **Byzantine-style church** built in British North America. A tragic fire in 1994 destroyed most of the wooden structure, but a national reconstruction campaign is currently underway.

Bishop Medley's Cathedral

In 1784 the new province of New Brunswick was created out of the northern part of Nova Scotia, so its not surprising that in 1845 New Brunswick was also granted its own Anglican diocese. Eight years later, the first entirely new British **cathedral** in North America was completed on Fredericton's riverfront park, The Green. Christ Church Cathedral was started by Rev. John Medley, who had arrived in 1845 from Exeter, England, to become the first Anglican Bishop of Fredericton. Under English ecclesiastical law, a new bishop seat could only be issued to a city. Despite a town population of only four thousand, Queen Victoria appointed Fredericton city status, and established a separate bishopric.

Bishop Medley copied the design for Christ Church from St Mary's Church in Snettisham and quarried the stone from Grindstone Island in Shepody Bay. Using the very best materials, including exotic woods, such as butternut, black walnut and ebony, construction slowly and painfully took place over the eight-year period as building funds were raised within the community. One anonymous gift for £500 was submitted by three ladies on

The Little Dutch Church in Halifax's north end, the first Lutheran Church in Canada. (L.B. Jenson)

the condition that the letters FSP were inscribed on the lower arch. Consecration was on August 31, 1853. Today, Christ Church Cathedral is considered one of the finest examples of Gothic architecture in North America. Bishop Medley spent over forty years travelling to many of the remote corners of his diocese before passing away in 1891.

Tallest Wooden Church

St. Mary's Church, next to Université Ste. Anne at Pointe de l'Église, Nova Scotia, is the **tallest wooden church** in North America. Completed in 1905, the church is noted for its collection of stained glass and was constructed in the form of a cross with the fifty-six metres (185 feet) high spire almost constantly in motion due to the strong winds of St. Mary's Bay. About thirty-six metric tons (40 tons) of ballast rock have been placed at the base of the steeple in order to keep the spire stable.

Trappist Monastery

In 1825, the first **Trappist monastery** in North America was built, mainly by the monks themselves, at Monastery, Nova Scotia. The seventy-room red brick building of the two hundred hectare (494 acre) retreat is a landmark in eastern Nova Scotia. Since 1938, the monastery has been operated by the Augustinian religious order, who also operate a mission in nearby Guysborough County.

Prior to World War II, the Augustinians fled Nazi Germany and the concentration camps as the borders closed. Seeking a Canadian refuge, they arrived in Monastery after hearing that the Trappist monks had abandoned their monastery. A Catholic religious order noted for their silence, the black-robed Augustinians greet each morning by chanting. Another Trappist monastery, currently run by two orders, including the Reformed Cistercians, is located in New Brunswick at Rogersville.

Social Rights

"Whereas no government of this Colony has yet done anything calculated to relieve the tenantry from the leasehold system underwhich we
are groaning. Therefore be it Resolved that the present union of tenants
is the only scheme yet adopted, likely to relieve us from proprietary
tyranny." — Establishment of the Tenant League of Prince Edward Island,
1864.

Divorce

The first official **divorce** in Canada was issued in 1750 at Halifax. At the
time, divorce under British law was considered a spiritual matter for the
church to consider, but with Halifax barely two years old, Governor Cornwallis' Executive Council was empowered to act as the Court of Judicature
and elected to also act as a Court of Matrimony and Divorce. The all-male
Court dealt cruelly, according to today's standards, with the female respon-
dent, Amy Williams.

Lieutenant William Williams was awarded an unanimous annulment
certificate with permission to marry again, while Amy Williams was found
guilty, forbidden to marry as long as the lieutenant was alive, and was ordered
to leave Nova Scotia within ten days.

Upon hearing of this dissolution proceeding, the London colonial
authorities expressed their disapproval of the non-ecclesiastical tribunal, but
in 1758 authorized the Nova Scotia Legislature to enact the first **Divorce
Statute** in Canada, empowering the governor's council to determine matters
of marriage and divorce.

/

Early Charities

Founded in 1768 in Halifax, the North British Society is the **oldest branch** of the charitable society outside Britain. Established to support local charities and cultural groups by a small group of Scottish merchants when Halifax was only nineteen years old, the society holds its annual gatherings each year to celebrate Scotland's most famous son, Robbie Burns, as well as to pipe in the haggis.

The **Canadian Charitable Irish Society** with Richard Bulkeley as president was founded in 1786 at Halifax, where the same year, the first German Society in Canada was also founded.

Race Riot

Canada's first known **racial conflict** occurred in 1784 at Shelburne, when a group of unemployed whites attacked the Black district of Birchtown destroying property and driving Blacks out of the area. The previous year about ten thousand Loyalists arrived at Shelburne, including 1,500 Black Loyalists, the first major **immigration of Blacks** into Canada. The Black Loyalists were denied land or given the least productive areas to farm, despite being promised equal treatment with other immigrants. Food and other provisions were provided to all Loyalists, yet many Blacks received only a fraction of the supplies issued to the white settlers.

The Shelburne area was unable to support such a large influx of people and while many of the white Loyalists moved on to more prosperous agricultural areas, the Blacks were unwilling to risk going back to slavery and began to accept low wages for whatever work was available. White labourers were affected and a group of mainly discharged soldiers attacked the Black community, destroying buildings and driving Blacks into the wilderness. Disillusioned with Nova Scotia and their treatment by the authorities, Blacks began to appeal to the British government for help.

In 1790, Thomas Peters, a community leader and Black Loyalist from Digby, travelled to London and was able to convince the British Colonial Office to arrange for 1,196 Black Loyalists, approximately one third of all Maritime Blacks, to move to Sierra Leone in West Africa, "free of expense," with full British rights and a promise of free land.

Waterfront Union

The 1840s were tough times in New Brunswick since British free trade made continued employment uncertain. Times were difficult especially for workers who had to compete for jobs against wave after wave of desperate European immigrants, particularly Irish-Catholics who escaped the potato famine in Ireland. Violence and strikes were not uncommon in Saint John as stevedores and other trades formed associations in order to cope with the turmoil of an anemic economy and the incoming cheap labour.

In 1849 Saint John had three unions formed within the space of seven weeks, including the Ships Carpenters' Society, Sawyers' Society, and the first **stevedores' union** in Canada, the Longshoremen's Labourers Society. About four hundred angry dock workers attended a public meeting demanding a shorter work week and a minimum daily wage of four shillings for unloading ships along Saint John's waterfront.

Their demand was met by the city's merchants and to commemorate the historic agreement, calling for a ten-hour workday at four shillings a day, a Labourers Bell was erected at the head of Market Slip with Saint John merchant, John Turnbull, ringing out the first public proclamation of the settlement. Now Saint John Local 273 of the International Longshoremen's Association, this historic waterfront union received its international charter in 1911.

The unions organized were defensive in nature, primarily New Brunswick-born Protestant workers joining together to protect their livelihood against the new Catholic immigrants who were anxious to establish themselves in the New World at almost any cost. While social violence in Saint John became less common after 1850, the struggle for employment opportunities between the orange and the green, Protestant and Catholic workers lasted almost a hundred years.

Island Tenant League

The first large-scale **tenant league** in Canada was organized in Prince Edward Island. In 1864 the league of small farmers pledged not to pay rent to absent landlords and to support other tenants who withheld their fees. This was done in order to force the estate owners to sell their land to the farmers at reasonable rates. From the earliest settlement of the British island colony, an extensive leasehold system of land had been established that granted large tracts of land to well-connected proprietors, but created discontent among their tenants.

In 1865, with a reported membership of eleven thousand, the league organized a march through Charlottetown of approximately five hundred protesters. One marcher, tenant farmer Sam Fletcher, was reportedly two years in rent arrears and was seized by police but managed to escape. Near Milton, Deputy Sheriff James Curtis and his bailiffs were attacked by pro-tenant sympathizers over a property dispute, resulting in a broken arm for Sheriff Curtis.

The countryside was very pro-tenant and violence became so rampant that troops were sent from Halifax to ensure order as well as to find Fletcher and the other resisters. Despite a £500 reward, Fletcher was never captured and became a popular symbol of resistance against the leaseholder land system. Two companies of the 2nd British Battalion remained on Prince Edward Island for eighteen months to maintain peace.

The Conservatives were defeated in 1867 on Prince Edward Island partly because of the Tenant League rebellion and slowly, land reform occurred despite the League's disappearance. Prince Edward Island agreed to enter Confederation in 1873 and was provided with federal funds to buy out the absent landowners and by 1895, the Land Question was largely settled with many tenants becoming property owners.

Now showing its age, the first credit union in Canada, The Farmer's Bank of Rustico.

The Farmer's Bank of Rustico

The forerunner of all North American credit unions is considered the large and successful La Caisse Populaire, established in 1901 at Levis, Quebec by Alphonse Desjardins. But Desjardins may have adopted the credit union idea from the Acadian farmers of the small Prince Edward Island community of Rustico. There the co-operative principles of people working together for community benefit were well in place almost forty years before the Quebec union established its first branch.

The Farmer's Bank of Rustico was founded in 1864, mainly through the efforts of the Acadian priest, George-Antoine Belcourt, who saw the need to become self-reliant when he said: "The farmer is the man who really creates wealth and bears the heaviest burden." Belcourt organized the local farmers into chartering a tiny people's bank with each farmer owning one share. This may well be the first **client-owned bank** in North America, designed and built by Father Belcourt and constructed from local sandstone.

Canada's smallest bank received official status and set its initial capital at the tiny sum of £800 sterling. With its conservative limit of two-to-one outstanding loans to on-hand capital, the Rustico Bank remained profitable, paying annual dividends of eight to ten per cent. The bank improved the economic situation of the farmers and actually survived, printing paper currency and lending money at generous rates. Extremely rare, Rustico Bank notes are now collector's items. The Canadian Bank Act forced the bank to close in 1894 since one condition imposed on all banks was a $500,000 cash reserve, far beyond the means of the tiny institution.

Now a National Historic Site Museum, the Farmer's Bank at South Rustico commemorates Father Belcourt's pioneering work. Efforts are currently underway to restore the aging structure. Today the Stella Maris Credit Union, which opened at Rustico in 1937, continues the Rustico tradition of community-based financial services established by Georges Belcourt. Father Belcourt established a parish library and boys school at Rustico and is claimed by the Rustico community to have constructed in 1866 the first **steam-operated automobile** on Prince Edward Island. He was also reported to have had the first car accident when his vehicle went off the road.

Coal Miners Union

Coal mining was an important source of employment and fuel throughout the Maritimes during the nineteenth century, especially Nova Scotia where thirty collieries were in operation in 1876. While the first **miners strike** in Canada occurred in 1840 at the Albion Mine in Pictou County, the earliest **coal miners trade union** in Canada was not incorporated until 1864, as the Albion Mines Union Association.

The coal miners union eventually became part of the Provincial Workman's Association of Nova Scotia (PWA), which secretly began organizing in 1879 in the woods outside Springhill. The secret association was initially called the Pioneer Lodge and was headed by Nova Scotia labour leader Robert Drummond. Born in Scotland and active in Scottish labour circles before immigrating to Nova Scotia, Drummond became the grand secretary of the PWA.

In an age when lodges of all sorts were flourishing, unions were modeled after fraternal orders and initially the PWA consisted of three union "lodges" from Pictou County and the Pioneer Lodge of Springhill. Eventually the PWA consisted of three sub-councils representing the three coal mining districts of Pictou, Cumberland and Cape Breton. A provincial act of incorporation soon gave the union an official status as well as legal standing.

Drummond led the coal workers for nineteen years through several strikes and lobbied government and the coal companies for improvements to the working conditions of the miners. He also published the union's journal but resigned as head of the union in 1898 after a rival American union raided the Nova Scotia association, virtually wiping it out. Drummond remained active in the coal industry until his death in 1925, writing and advising the provincial government on coal mining issues.

First YWCA Chapter

The **Young Women's Christian Association** was founded in Canada in 1870 on Saint John's Germain Street by Anne A. Blizzard. Begun in Canada as an off-shoot of the New England organization, the association was interested in creating educational and employment opportunities for young women. While its constitution's stated objective was the "mutual spiritual improvement of its members," the association was inter-denominational, largely concerned with the physical well-being of the many young women moving into industrial cities like Saint John. The committee of about ten women, including Miss Blizzard, established a shelter for homeless girls as well as a program of social work, including prayer meetings and weekly visits to women in hospitals, homes, and jails.

The YWCA was started in England to help accommodated the large number of single women entering the British industrialized cities of the mid-1800s. The national organization for all of Canada was created later in 1895 at a national convention in Ottawa and by World War I, there were twenty-six chapters across Canada.

Co-operatives and the Antigonish Movement

Co-operative organizations are usually considered to be enterprises owned and operated for the purposes of its members. The first **co-operative society** organized in Canada was reported to be a miners stable store that was opened in 1861 at Stellarton. An Acadian Co-operative Society was also incorporated in 1871 at Westville, Pictou County, under co-operative principles. Other co-operatives began to appear in Cape Breton, Prince Edward

Island, and elsewhere in the late 1800s, including the organized grain co-operatives, the forerunners to today's food marketing boards.

Besides adult education, co-operatives were the other innovative component of what is today known as the **Antigonish Movement**. The Cape Breton cousins that were largely responsible for teaching communities how to help themselves by organizing co-operatives to process and market their own products, were both born in Cape Breton, became Roman Catholic priests, and began their work in the 1920s at St. Francis Xavier University in Antigonish. The radical Jimmy Tompkins, who founded the People's School at St. Francis, was determined to transfer learning to the common man but became a controversial figure and was banished to Canso. In 1935, however, near Reserve Mines, Tompkins managed to help establish the first **co-operative housing project** in Canada, called Tompkinsville, and also started a credit union, as well as one of the earliest **regional libraries** in the Maritimes.

Moses Coady became the first director of the Extension Program at St. Francis Xavier and taught evening classes throughout eastern Nova Scotia, pushing his message that control of local communities through credit unions and co-operatives held the key to revitalizing the economically depressed Maritimes. He organized the Nova Scotia Teacher's Union as well as assisted establishment of the United Maritime Fishermen's Union. Coady's two books, *Masters Of Their Own Destiny* and *The Man From Margaree* are still widely read today. Coady died at Antigonish in 1959, and within a few months, the **Coady International Institute** was established at St. Francis to encourage Third World students to study the Coady-Tompkins ideals for community development through cooperation, self-reliance, and education.

National Black Coalition

Carrie Best was born in 1903 in New Glasgow and devoted her life to helping women and young people, especially Blacks, acquire a sense of identity, integrity and pride of race. In 1973, she received the first annual award of the **National Black Coalition** of Canada, recognizing her life's work as a human rights organizer. In 1946 she help found the bi-weekly *Clarion*, the first **newspaper for Blacks** in Nova Scotia. Its goal was to provide a voice for "coloured Nova Scotians for promoting inter-racial understanding and good will." Best also issued *The Negro Citizen* in 1949 and narrated her own radio program.

In 1974 she was made a member of the Order of Canada and later found time to write as well as self-publish her autobiography, *That Lonesome Road*. Considered a milestone in detailing underprivileged life for Maritime Blacks, Best describes her biography as "a permanent record of a journey down a lonesome road in search of an identity, where, like a fool, I sometimes rushed in where angels feared to tread."

Police Union and Strike

The first **paid police force** in Canada was established in Saint John in 1826 when city fathers advertised they were willing to receive tenders for hiring six men "for the nightly watch." Lawlessness and the city's rapid growth had meant that citizens militia and British troops were no longer adequate for policing needs. The city's Common Council also insisted a £50 bond be paid per policeman to ensure the "faithful performance of duty."

Saint John's turbulent past and strong labour tradition manifested itself in 1918 when the first **police union** in Canada was organized. Canada was experiencing massive economic change in the early twentieth century. Workers were rapidly unionizing and clashing with employers yet most police were also working-class wage earners and were expected to control disgruntled labourers. Disgruntled themselves with poor wages and working conditions, over half of Saint John's police met at the Elks Club and formed the Saint John Police Protective Association, applying for a charter with the national Labour Congress.

Fear of affiliation with radical local unions and cries of German propaganda and Bolshevism, led the Commissioner of Public Safety, H. R. McLellan, to dismiss all unionized officers despite their willingness to submit their proposed bylaws for his approval. Tensions rose as the lock-out polarized Saint John with widespread support for the officers coming from police forces throughout Canada.

A subsequent election voted McLellan out of office and the new commissioner reinstated the dismissed officers, while a federal conciliation board granted the police officers the right to form associations and affiliate with national labour organizations. The board did oppose any link with local labour groups in order to try and maintain a separation between police and the Saint John labour movement. A joint city and police union grievance commission was established, and with dues set at fifty cents, Canada first police brotherhood was instituted.

The first **legal police strike** in Canadian history occurred in 1971 at Sydney, Cape Breton. Some minor looting and disorder took place as the police withdrew their services. The fifty-six man Sydney police force had accepted a conciliation board's recommended thirty per cent increase over three years but the city would only offer fifteen per cent over two years. In 1971, a first-class Sydney constable earned an annual income of $6,500.

While on strike, the police continued to provide emergency service but after rowdyism and open drinking occurred on Charlotte Street, leaving a dozen stores with broken windows and damaged merchandise, citizens began to fear Sydney was becoming wide open. Within twenty-four hours, Nova Scotia's Attorney General Leonard Pace intervened and persuaded the mayor and city council to accept the conciliation board's wage proposal. The city police went on strike again in 1984 but the RCMP immediately took over the policing of Sydney.

Military

"I will take the chances." — Able Seamen William Hall volunteering for a near fatal mission at the Relief of Lucknow, which he survived and was awarded the Victoria Cross for bravery.

National Historic Fort

Fort Anne at Annapolis Royal became Canada's first **National Historic Park** in 1917. Built originally in 1687 by French forces, the earthworks fortifying the site were actually constructed in 1635. Captured by British troops under Francis Nicholson in 1710, the fort was renamed Fort Anne in honour of Queen Anne. The fort reflects the early British colonial period and includes the British officers' quarters as well as the dreaded black hole dungeon. Garrisoned with British troops until 1854, Fort Anne is now a fully restored twelve hectare (30 acre) park and a major tourist attraction in Annapolis Royal.

Walled Town

While Quebec City is considered the oldest existing walled city in North America, its fortifications, while begun prior to the founding of Louisbourg, were actually completed around the city after Louisbourg had been built. The first **completed walled town** in North America, Louisbourg, was constructed between 1719 and 1744, serving as France's Atlantic fortress after the 1713 Treaty of Utrecht had ceded Newfoundland and Acadia to Britain but allowed Ile Royale (Cape Breton) to remain a French possession. Initially erected as a base for France's important cod fishery, Louisbourg developed into one of the busiest seaports in North America and the centre of French power along the Atlantic coast.

Louisbourg was constructed by Jean-François Verville according to French fortification principles of the eighteenth century which called for low, six metres (20 feet) thick, bastion walls to protect against cannon fire. A huge complex when completed, Louisbourg comprised almost forty hectares (100 acres) within its walls and was surrounded by a twenty-four metre (80 feet) wide moat.

The King's Bastion Barracks, built at great expense, was the **largest building** in North America when completed around 1740. The interior town was marked off in rectangular blocks, unlike early American street designs, and as a fully fortified town, was considered a "tough nut to crack" by American Benjamin Franklin. Crack it did, first in 1745 and finally in 1758, after being besieged by British and New England forces estimated at about twenty-seven thousand men. The fortress was demolished and the population disbursed. Today, Louisbourg is a National Historic Site and Canada's largest reconstructed outdoor museum with about one quarter of the original town restored.

Oldest Blockhouse

The **oldest military blockhouse** still surviving in Canada is the small split log Fort Edward at Windsor, Nova Scotia. Erected by Major Lawrence in 1750 to control the Acadian presence in the region, the fort was one of the main assembly points during the 1755 Expulsion of the Acadians. The site overlooking the Avon River was then called Piziquid and today the fort is still surrounded by a moat with cannons facing the river. Fort Edward once contained eighty cannons and a garrison of 168 men and eight officers. It also housed officers quarters, soldiers barracks, a hospital for twenty-six patients, stables and other buildings. Today, only the blockhouse remains. Garrisoned by British troops for over a century, the fortifications were dismantled and troops withdrawn during the nineteenth century.

A famous Scottish heroine from the Battle of Culloden, Flora MacDonald, spent the winter of 1779 at Fort Edward with her husband, Captain Alan MacDonald, who commanded a detachment of Highland Emigrants. Arrested and tried for aiding the Jacobite cause by helping Bonnie Prince Charlie to escape from the British army, Flora MacDonald was allowed to live in exile in North Carolina and returned to her Isle of Skye home after eighteen months at Windsor. The Fort Edward blockhouse was restored in 1956 and is now a National Historic Site administrated by Parks Canada.

First Martello Tower

At Point Pleasant Park on the tip of the Halifax peninsula stands the first **Martello tower** constructed in the British Empire. A French defensive innovation first encountered by British forces at Corsica during the Napoleonic Wars, the Martello fort was considered impregnable against conventional military equipment of the period. Called the Prince of Wales Tower, it introduced North America to this new defense structure and was built between 1796 and 1799 as a coastal defence tower to protect British sea batteries at Point Pleasant against possible French attacks.

Constructed of ironstone by Prince Edward, Duke of Kent, and the Commanding Royal Engineer, Captain James Straton, the tower overlooks the entrance to Halifax harbour as well as the passage up the Northwest Arm. Featuring 2.5 metre (8 feet) thick walls at the base, the round tower was built to withstand heavy cannon fire, and includes three gun ports on the second storey. The tower was built on the highest ground in the park to command the best view of the harbour and became a key defense to the Halifax Harbour approaches. Over the next forty years, 136 more such towers were built throughout Britain and Canada, including four more in the Halifax defense system.

Prince Edward's Telegraph System

During the Napoleonic era, Halifax became the British military centre in North America serving to challenge French interests as well as their American allies. Often considered Halifax's golden period as a naval port, the city's importance in Britain was heightened when in 1794, King George's son, Prince Edward, was appointed Commander-in-Chief of Nova Scotia. The Prince was energetic and competent in military affairs. Besides the Martello tower project, the Prince of Wales made many important improvements to the Halifax defensive complex during his six years residence.

Keenly interested in military innovations, Edward introduced the new French **semaphore telegraph system** to North America. French success in the early years of the Napoleonic Wars was partly the result of the Cappe brothers' visual telegraphy system whereby brief military messages could be sent hundreds of miles in mere minutes. By devising a similar signalling system with flags, wickerwork, drums, and even lanterns at night, Edward's engineers established a military communication network from Chebucto Head at the mouth of Halifax harbour, to Citadel Hill, and throughout the entire military installations around Halifax. Edward became so pleased with his telegraph system that he extended the signalling stations to Windsor and Annapolis Royal. A Halifax to Windsor message was capable of being received in twenty minutes.

Prince Edward was convinced an unbroken communication line could be established throughout Canada. Each station was erected on high ground about twelve kilometres (7.5 miles) apart. Stations were established to Saint John and up the Saint John River as far as Fredericton with plans to proceed to Quebec. Yet few, if any, visual signals seem to have been sent to New Brunswick, since by this time Prince Edward had returned to England. Except around Halifax and Saint John, the visual telegraph system was not maintained and even dismantled in places, perhaps because of its massive manpower requirements. The Maritimes would have to wait almost fifty years for Morse's electric telegraph to invade the region in a more cost-effective manner.

William Hall, V.C.

The first Canadian sailor as well as the first Black to receive the **Victoria Cross** for bravery was Nova Scotian William E. Hall. Born in 1826 at Horton Bluff, near Hantsport, Hall was the son of a Black slave from Virginia who immigrated to Nova Scotia during the War of 1812. After serving in the merchant service and the United States Navy, Hall joined the Royal Navy in 1852, and served briefly on Nelson's flagship *Victory*, receiving an award for bravery during the Crimean War.

Hall was aboard *HMS Shannon* in 1857 during the Indian Mutiny and volunteered to help drag the ship's guns across the countryside and endured heavy fire attempting to breach through the walled town of Lucknow. He was left alone with one wounded officer but managed to single-handedly maintain fire and penetrate the thick walls, allowing re-enforcements through to rescue the British defenders trapped inside.

Hantsport Baptist Church —
Grave & Memorial of William Hall, Victoria Cross,
the first Negro & one of the first Canadians to
win this honour. Won as an Able Seaman RN from
HMS Shannon during the Indian Mutiny in 1857.

William Hall Memorial: Grave and memorial at Hantsport Baptist Church of Canadian hero William Hall, first Canadian seaman to receive the Victoria Cross for Bravery. (L.B. Jenson)

The Relief of Lucknow during the Indian Mutiny is well known to British school children and Hall's heroic action against overwhelming odds resulted in him receiving the highest honour for valour. On October 30, 1859, aboard his ship, the *Donegal*, Hall was awarded the Victoria Cross, the most famous medal of wartime bravery, by Rear-Admiral Charles Talbot.

Hall later served in China and retired from the British Navy in 1876, after almost twenty years of service and four medals for bravery. He returned to his small farm near Hantsport where he died in 1904. Buried without honours in an unmarked grave at Lockhartville, recognition of this Canadian hero came posthumously through the efforts of members of the Canadian Legion. Today, Hall is buried on the lawn of the Hantsport Baptist Church with a hand-carved replica of the Victoria Cross overhead. A Royal Canadian Legion branch in Halifax is named in his honour.

Aerial Photography

The earliest **aerial photographs** in Canada were taken in Halifax in 1883 by Captain Henry Elsdale of the Royal Engineers. Stationed with the Imperial Garrison, after having worked with the original British Army ballooning school at Woolwich, England, Elsdale pursued his experiments in air photography above the Halifax Citadel with the assistance of the Royal Engineers.

Unmanned military balloons had been in use for some time in Europe in order to make runs over disputed areas or to spy above enemy lines. By the 1880s, even bombs had been dropped from balloons. At his own expense, Elsdale had devised a small balloon with a plate type camera suspended below the balloon and fitted with an automatic shutter-release that was operated by clockwork. Aerial photographs from the period still exist and reveal the military installations clustered around the Citadel.

Captain Elsdale also developed a complicated **free balloon system** whereby he could calculate its retrieval point. The scheme involved fitting the balloon camera with a device that once the desired photographs were taken, would let the gas out of the balloon at a rate calculated to allow the balloon to drop at the predicted place. A pioneer in the use of air photography for military purposes, Captain Elsdale returned to England in 1884 and resumed his work with the British school of ballooning.

World War I Ace

World War I firmly established the military significance of air power and the importance of the new flying machines. Although Canada did not have an air force of its own until the 1920s, a significant number of early flying "aces" (pilots with five or more kills) were Canadians flying with the British Royal Flying Services. The first **Allied pilot** to shoot down one of Germany's feared Gotha bombers was Alberton, PEI native Wendell W. Rogers.

Rogers enlisted with the Royal Flying Corps in 1916 and displayed unusual flying talent over the Western Front, becoming an ace pilot in eighteen months. His celebrity status was assured in late 1917 when he led four Allied pilots on a patrol over Armentieres and encountered the giant enemy Gotha bombers. Designed to destroy Britain, the long-range Gotha seemed indestructible with its five hundred-horsepower engines, high cruising altitude, and the ability to fly at considerable speed for almost four hours. Flying the single-seater Nieuport Scout, with one machine gun mounted over the wing, Rogers and two other Scouts attacked. Rogers zoomed in under a Gotha's tail and fired sixty rounds, hitting the plane's petrol tank and sending it exploding to the ground.

Captain Wendell Rogers received the Military Cross for being the first to bring down a Gotha bomber. In all, he became an ace twice over by registering ten enemy kills in less than two years of flying action. In the last year of World War I, Rogers returned to Canada and became a flying instructor and squadron commander.

Naval College

The Canadian Navy, a distinct entity from the Royal Navy, came into existence in 1910 and the **Royal Naval College** of Canada opened its doors in Halifax the next year. Situated in the old hospital building in the Dockyard, the college began graduating Canadian **naval cadets** in 1913. While the curriculum was similar to British naval colleges, the facility was under Canadian command and a number of the early Canadian **naval casualties** of World War I were trainees of the college. The Halifax Explosion of 1917 damaged the college building and the cadets were initially transferred to Kingston, Ontario, and finally in 1918, the college was moved permanently to Esquimalt, BC.

Naval Convoy

During World War II, a reported 17,593 ships sailed in convoy formation across the Atlantic, supplying the Allies with vital military and civilian goods in order to continue the war effort. No port was more essential to these fleets of merchant ships than Halifax and on September 16, 1939, the first **naval convoy** consisting of eighteen ships and escorted by *HMCS St. Laurent* and *Saguenay*, assembled in Bedford Basin, quit Halifax harbour, and sailed to England.

The Halifax naval dockyard, established in 1759 as His Majesty's Naval Yard, was the first official **British dockyard** in Canada. Captain James Cook supervised the erection of the first buildings while stationed there in 1759. The King's Yard underwent a huge expansion during World War II and by

1945, the yard had developed into a large and modern marine facility while the Royal Canadian Navy had expanded from thirteen warships and three hundred men to 365 warships with 100,000 naval personnel. Allied convoys also sailed from the Maritime ports of Sydney and Saint John.

Female Naval Commanders

The first and only female in the Canadian Navy to **command a ship** during World War II was Commander Isabel Janet MacNeil of Halifax. Born in Halifax in 1908, MacNeil attended the Halifax Ladies College, Mount Saint Vincent University, as well as Dalhousie University, and became commanding officer of the Women's Royal Canadian Naval Service, responsible for training over six thousand recruits. She commanded *HMCS Conestoga* and became the first **WRENS officer** to be decorated when she received the Order of the British Empire in 1944. MacNeil also received the Order of Canada and besides her assistance in establishing the RCN Wrens, became involved in women's penal reform work.

Colonel Sheila Hellstrom of Nova Scotia became the first **female brigadier-general** in Canada in January 1987. Hellstrom joined the RCAF in 1954 and is credited with working throughout her career to increase the number of women in the ranks of the Canadian military.

Bibliography

Acheson, T.W. *Saint John: The Making Of A Colonial Urban Community.* University of Toronto Press, 1985.

Akins, Thomas Beamish. *History of Halifax.* Mika Publishing, 1973.

Armour, Charles A., and Thomas Lackey. *Sailing Ships of The Maritmes.* McGraw-Hill Ryerson, 1975.

Arnell, J.C. *Atlantic Mails.* National Postal Museum, 1980.

Baglole, Harry. *Exploring Island History.* Ragweed Press, 1977.

Baird, Frank. T. *Story of Fredericton.* Amos Wilson, 1948.

Balcom, B.A. *History of the Lunenburg Fishing Industry.* Lunenburg Marine Museum Society,

Baldwin, Douglas. *Land of the Red Soil.* Ragweed, 1990.

Barkhouse, Murray. *Famous Nova Scotians.* Lancelot Press, 1994.

Barnard, Murray. *Nova Scotia Legislature.* Province of Nova Scotia, 1979.

Baseball Encyclopedia, 8th Edition. Macmillan Publishing, 1990.

Bates, George T. "Some Seal Island Shipwrecks." *Nova Scotia Historical Quarterly,* Volume I # 1

Bell, D.G. *Early Loyalist Saint John.* New Ireland Press, 1983.

Bell, Winthrop Pickard. *Foreign Protestants and the Settlement of Nova Scotia.* University of Toronto Press, 1961.

Blakeley, Phyllis, R. "Theatre and Music in Halifax." *Dalhousie Review,* April, 1949.

———. "William Hall, Canada's First Naval V.C." *Dalhousie Review,* Volume XXXVII, 1957-58.

Bliss, Michael. *Northern Enterprise.* McClelland & Stewart, 1987.

Braithwaite, Rolla, and Tessa Benn-Ireland. *Some Black Women.* Sister Vision, 1993.

Brebner, John Bartlett. *Neutral Yankees of Nova Scotia.* McClelland & Stewart, 1969.

Brown, J.J. *Ideas In Exile.* McClelland & Stewart, 1967.

———. *Inventors, Great Ideas in Canadian Enterprise.* McClelland & Stewart, 1967.

Bruce, Robert, V. *Alexander Graham Bell and the Conquest of Solitude.* Little, Brown and Company, 1973.

Cameron, James M. *More About Pictonians*. Lancelot Press, 1983.

———. *Pictonian Colliers*. Nova Scotia Museum, 1974.

———. *Pictou County's History*. Pictou County Historical Society, 1972.

Canadian Encyclopedia, Second Edition. Hurtig Publishers, 1988.

Cassidy, Ivan. *Nova Scotia: All About Us*. Nelson Canada. 1983.

Cheaka, Alyce Taylor. "Antigonish Highland Games." *Nova Scotia Historical Review*, Volume 3, # 1, 1983.

Clandfield, David. *Canadian Film*. Oxford University Press, 1987.

Clark, Andrew. *Acadia: The Geography Of Early Nova Scotia to 1760*. University of Wisconsin Press, 1968.

Clarke, George Elliott. *Fire On The Water, Volume 1*. Pottersfield Press, 1991.

Conrad, Margaret. *They Planted Well*. Acadiensis Press, 1988.

———. *Too Soon the Curtain Fell*. Brunswick Press, 1981.

De Volpi, Charles P. *Montreal: A Pictorial Record, Volume I*. Longman Canada, 1963.

———. *Nova Scotia, A Pictorial Record*. Longman Canada, 1974.

———. *Newfoundland: A Pictorial Record*. Longman Canada, 1972.

Denys, Nicholas. *Description and Natural History of the Coasts of North America (Acadia)*. Edited by Ganong, W.F. Champlain Society, 1908.

Doyle, Arthur. *Front Benches & Back Rooms*. Green Tree Publishing, 1976.

Doyle, Arthur T. *Heroes of New Brunswick*. Brunswick Press, 1984.

Dunlop, Alan C." Pharmacist and Entrepreneur — Pictou's J.D.B. Fraser." *Nova Scotia Historical Quarterly*, Volume N, #1, 1974.

Eber, Dorothy Harley. *Genius At Work*. Nimbus Publishing, 1991.

Elliott, Shirley B. *Nova Scotia Book of Days*. Province of Nova Scotia, 1979.

Fergusson, Bruce   . *Charles Fenerty*. William Macnab & Son, 1955.

Fergusson. C. Bruce. "Halifax Post Office." *Dalhousie Review*, Volume XXXVIII, 1958-59.

———. "Rise of the Theatre in Halifax." *Dalhousie Review*, January, 1950.

Fergusson, Charles Bruce. *William Hall, V.C. Nova Scotia Journal of Education,* December, 1967.

Fetherling, Douglas. *Documents in Canadian Film*. Broadview Press, 1990.

———. *Rise of the Canadian Newspaper*. University of Oxford Press. 1990.

Fitsell, J.W. *Hockey's Captains, Colonels, & Kings*. Boston Mills Press, 1987.

Flemming, Horace A. "Halifax Currency." *Collections of the Nova Scotia Historical Society*, Volume XX, 1921.

Flick, Don. "Early Money in Nova Scotia." *Nova Scotia Historical Review*, Volume I, #2, 1981.

Flood, Brian. *Saint John A Sporting Tradition 1785-1985*. Neptune Publishing, 1985.

Folster, David. *Chocolate Ganongs of St. Stephen, New Brunswick*. Macmillan of Canada, 1990.

Ford, Karen, J. Maclean, and B. Wansbrough. *Great Canadian Lives: Portraits in Heroism to 1867*. Nelson Canada, 1985.

Forester, Joseph, and Anne Forester. *Silver Fox Odessey*. Canadian Silver Fox Breeders Association, 1980.

Friends of the Public Gardens. *Halifax Public Gardens*. Friends of the Public Gardens, 1989.

Gair, Reavley. *Literary and Linguistic History of New Brunswick*. Goose Lane Editions, 1985.

Ganong, William Francis. *Champlain's Island*. New Brunswick Museum, 1945.

Gordon, Grant. *From Slavery To Freedom:The Life of David George*. Lancelot Press, 1992.

Grant, John N. *Black Nova Scotians*. Nova Scotia Museum, 1984.

———. *Immigration & Settlement of the Black Refugees of the War of 1812 in Nova Scotia & New Brunswick*.

Grayson, Stan. *Old Marine Engines*. Devereux Books, 1994.

Greer, Rosamand. *Girls of the King's Navy*. Sono Nis Press, 1983.

Hacker, Carlotta. *Book Of Canadians*. Hurtig Publishers, 1983.

Halifax Library Association. *Nova Scotia in Books 1752-1967*. Nova Scotia Provincial Library, 1967.

Halpenny, Frances, ed. *Dictionary of Canadian Biography*. University of Toronto Press, 1974.

Harper, J. Rusell. *Painting in Canada: A History*. University of Toronto Press, 1966.

———. "Theatre in Saint John, 1789-1817." *Dalhousie Review*, Autumn, 1954.

Harshaw, Josephine Perfect. *When Women Work Together*. Ryerson Press, 1966.

Hocking, Anthony. *Prince Edward Island*. McGraw-Hill Ryerson, 1978.

Jack, David Russell. "Early Journalism in New Brunswick." *Acadiensis*, Volume VIII, 1908.

Jephcott, C.M. *Postal History of Nova Scotia and New Brunswick*. Sissons Publications, 1964.

Johnson, Ralph. *Forests of Nova Scotia*. Four East Publications, 1986.

Johnstone, Kenneth. *Aquatic Explorers*. University of Toronto Press, 1977.

Jones, Elizabeth. *Gentlemen and Jesuits*. University of Toronto Press, 1986.

Kane, Joseph Nathan. *Famous First Facts*. H.W. Wilson Company, 1981.

Kennedy, Earle. *P.E.I. Holey Dollar*. Willaim & Crue, 1976.

MacBeath, George, and Donald F. Taylor. *Steamboat Days*. Print'N Press, 1982.

MacGillivray, Allister. *Diamonds In The Rough, 25 Years With The Men Of The Deeps*. Men of the Deeps Music, 1991.

MacKay, Donald. *Scotland Farewell*. McGraw-Hill Ryerson, 1980.

MacKean, Ray, and Robert Percival. *Little Boats*. Brunswick Press, 1979.

Maclaren, George. *Pictou Book*. Hector Publishing, 1954.

MacLean, R.A. *State of Mind, The Scots in Nova Scotia*. Lancelot Press, 1992.

Macleod, Carol. *Glimpses Into New Brunswick History*. Lancelot Press, 1984.

MacNutt, W.S. *New Brunswick: A History: 1784-1867*. Macmillan of Canada, 1984.

Major, Marjorie. "Andrews Downs." *Nova Scotia Historical Quarterly*, Volume 1, #2, June 1971.

Manchester, Lorne. *Canada's Fisheries*. McGraw-Hill, 1970.

Marble, Allan. *Nova Scotians at Home and Abroad*. Lancelot Press, 1986.

Marble, Allan Everett. *Surgeons Smallpox and the Poor*. McGill-Queen's University Press, 1993.

Martin, John Patrick. *Story of Dartmouth*, John P. Martin, 1981.

McCreath, Peter L., and John G. Leefe. *History of Early Nova Scotia*. Four East Publications, 1982.

McGuigan, Peter. "Tenants and Troopers." *The Island*, Fall/Winter, 1992.

McNeil, Mary. *Blind Knight of Nova Scotia*. University Press, 1939.

Mellor, John. *Company Store*. Doubleday Canada, 1983.

Morell, Marjorie Taylor. *Mines and Miners*. Minto, N.B., 1981.

Morrison, J. Clinton Jr. "Death From Above." *The Island*, #22, Fall/Winter, 1987.

Mowat, Grace Helen. *Diverting History of a Loyalist Town*. Brunswick Press, 1953.

Myers, Jay. *Canadian Facts & Dates*. Fitzhenry & Whiteside, 1991.

Nader, Ralph, N. Milleron, and D. Conacher. *Canada Firsts*. McClelland & Stewart, 1992.

Newton, Pamela. *Cape Breton Book of Days*. University College of Cape Breton Press, 1984.

Nova Scotia Department of Agriculture and Marketing. *Maritime Dykelands*. 1987.

Nova Scotia Department of Natural Resources. *One of the Greatest Treasures, The Geology & History of Coal in Nova Scotia*. 1993.

Pacey, Elizabeth, and Alvin Comiter. *Historic Halifax*. Hounslow Press, 1988.

Parker, George. *Beginning of the Book Trade in Canada*. University of Toronto Press, 1985.

Patterson, George. *History of the County of Pictou*. Mika, 1972.

Payzant, Joan, and Lewis Payzant. *Like a Weaver's Shuttle*. Nimbus Publishing, 1979.

Peck, Mary. *Bitter With the Sweet New Brunswick 1604-1984*. Four East Publications, 1983.

Perkins, Charlotte Isabella. *Romance of Old Annapolis Royal Nova Scotia*. Historical Association of Annapolis Royal, 1934.

Phillips, Fred. *Fredericton, the Early Years*. New Brunswick Archives, 1980.

Piers, Harry. "Artists In Nova Scotia." *Collections of the Nova Scotia Historical Society*, Volume XVIII, 1914.

Plaskett, William. *Lunenburg, An Inventory of Historic Buildings*. Town of Lunenburg, 1984.

Post, Robert. *Tancook Whalers*. Maine Maritime Museum, 1985.

Punch, Terrence M. *Some Sons of Erin in Nova Scotia*. Petheric Press, 1980.

Quinpool, John. *First Things in Acadia*. First Things Publishers, 1936.

Raddall, Thomas H. *Halifax Warden of the North*. McClelland & Stewart, 1971.

———. "Nova Scotia's First Telegraph System." *Dalhousie Review*, Volume XXVII #2, July, 1947.

Rankin, Robert Allan. *Down At The Shore*. Prince Edward Island Heritage Foundation, 1980.

Rankin, Allan. "Mister Hall's Machines." *The Island*, #8,1980.

Rawlyk, G.A. *Ravished by the Spirit*. McGill-Queens University Press, 1984.

Regan, John W. *Sketches And Traditions of the Northwest Arm*. Hounslow Press, 1978.

Reid, John. *Mount Allison University Volume I: 1843-1914*. University of Toronto Press, 1984.

———. "Education of Women at Mount Allison 1845-1914." *Acadiensis*, Volume XII, #2, Spring, 1983.

Reid, John G. *Six Crucial Decades*. Nimbus Publishing, 1987.

Robertson, Barbara R. *Sawpower*. Nimbus/NSM, 1986.

Robinson, Charlotte. *Pioneer Profiles of New Brunswick Settlers*. Mika Publishing, 1980.

Ross, Sally, and Alphonse Deveau. *Acadians Of Nova Scotia Past and Present*. Nimbus Publishing 1992.

Ryan, Judith Hoegg. *Coal In Our Blood*. Formac Publishing, 1992.

Sadlier, Rosemary. *Leading The Way: Black Women in Canada*. Umbrella Press, 1994.

Scala, Alexander. *Treasures of Canada*. Samuel-Stevens, Publishers 1980.

Schuyler, George. *Saint John, Scenes From a Popular History*. Petheric Press, 1984.

See, Scott W. *Riots in New Brunswick*. University of Toronto Press, 1993.

Senn, Roma. "Zwickers." *Atlantic Insight*, 1982.

Shand, Gwendolyn. *Historic Hants County*. Petheric Press, 1979.

Sherwood, Roland H. *Pictou Pioneers*. Lancelot Press,1973.

Smith, Rankine M. *History of Basketball in New Brunswick, Canada*. Royal Printing, 1991.

Spicer, Stanley T. *Masters of Sail*. Petheric Press, 1982.

Spray, W.A. *Blacks in New Brunswick*. Brunswick Press, 1972.

Squires, Austin. *History of Fredericton The Last 200 Years*. City of Fredericton, 1980.

Stanley, Della M. *Louis Robichaud: A Decade of Power*. Nimbus Publishing, 1984.

Stelmok, Jerry, and RollinThurlow. *Wood & Canvas Canoe*. Old Bridge Press, 1987.

Stewart, Dr. W. Brenton. *Medicine in New Brunswick*. New Brunswick Medical Society, 1974.

Swanick, Eric L. *New Brunswick History*. New Brunswick Legislative Library, 1984.

Taylor, Graham D., and Peter A. Baskerville. *Concise History of Business in Canada*. Oxford

Toward, Lilias M. *Mabel Bell*. Methuen, 1984.

Tratt, Gertrude E.N. *Nova Scotia Newspapers 1752-1957*. Dalhousie University Libraries, 1979.

Tweedie, R. A., Fred Cogswell, and Stewart MacNutt. *Arts In New Brunswick*. University Press of New Brunswick, 1967.

Vroom, Richard, and Arthur Doyle. *Old New Brunswick*. Oxford University Press, 1978.

Walker, Willa. *No Hay Fever & A Railway*. Goose Lane Editions, 1989.

Wallace, Frederick William. *Wooden Ships and Iron Men*. White Lion Publishers, 1973.

Wallace, Gerald, William Higgins, and Peter McGahan. *Saint John Police Story, Volume 2*. New Ireland Press, 1992.

Walsh, Dr. Patrick F. *History of Antigonish*. Casket Printing, 1989.

Webster, J. Clarence. *Historical Guide to New Brunswick*. New Brunswick Government, 1930.

White, G.A. *Halifax And Its Business*. Nova Scotia Printing Company, 1876.

Whitehead, Ruth Holmes. *Elitekey Micmac Material Culture*. Nova Scotia Museum, 1980.

———. *Old Man Told Us: Excerpts from Micmac History 1500-1950*. Nimbus, 1991.

Wilson, Bruce G.. *Colonial Identities*. National Archives, 1988.

Wright, Esther Clark. *Saint John Ships and Their Builders*. Wolfville, 1975.

Wright, Harold, and Rob Roy. *Saint John and The Fundy Region*. Neptune Publishing, 1987.

Wynn, Graeme. *Timber Colony*. University of Toronto Press, 1981.

Young, A.J. Sandy. *Beyond Heroes: A Sport History Of Nova Scotia Vol. I &II*. Lancelot Press, 1988.

Index

E

D

F